CONSUMED

40 Days
of Fasting, Repentance & Rebirth

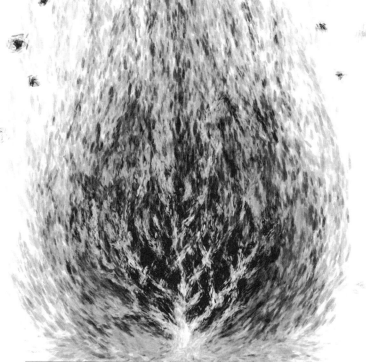

DEAN BRIGGS

CHAMPIC

D1277351

Consumed
40 Days of Fasting, Repentance & Rebirth

Cover images courtesy of Dreamstime.com.
Cover design by Barkely & Co.
Book design by Eugenia Brock.

ISBN-13: 978-0692363614
ISBN-10: 0692363610

First Printing—January 2015
Printed in the United States of America

CONTENTS

FOREWORD

A few years ago, I experienced a perfect storm of the soul. Within a three week period, three major life-sapping events occurred. First, after battling a long, chronic illness, I was finally forced to resort to major surgery, which left me scarred both physically and figuratively. A week later my daughter married a wonderful Aussie man and moved 8,000 miles away. Finally, a week after the wedding, I was in full production mode for a new, live worship album. Several rounds of rehearsals followed on a tight schedule. These sessions with the band, singers, and orchestra were both wonderful and exhausting.

The net effect took a huge physical and emotional toll. By the end of it all, I felt overwhelmed, badly depleted, and ready to throw in the towel . . . until I discovered this book.

Dean sent me the manuscript to review. I've been privileged to walk through life with this mighty man of faith for several years now. Even so, when he asked me to read *Consumed*, I was hesitant. Fasting sounded impossible to me in my current emotional state, and I was afraid he would ask me to commit to one. Though he didn't, something caused my heart to leap toward the idea anyway. As I began reading the book, the Lord began to soften me to the idea of actually attempting a full, 40-day fast. By the second day's reading I was intrigued enough to give it a go. More than that, I felt deeply encouraged. (Hint: you will be, too!)

Even so, I was bluntly honest with the Lord. "I do not see how I can do this, Father. Are you really calling me to a fast?" His reply: *"Son, you need it. I want you to reboot your system."*

I knew immediately what He meant. Just as computers build up malware, viruses and junk software that bloats the core system and bogs down performance, as well as exposing it to various dangers, I instantly understood that my software needed a good cleansing. Little did I know but He was about to take me on one of the most incredible journeys of my life!

As soon as I mentally made the decision to begin, I asked the Lord for grace to follow through for all forty days. His response was immediate: *"As you meditate on my Word, I will give you a song a day from your meditations. You are then to record each day's song that same day. You will find encouragement for your soul in the process. My grace will be more than enough to sustain you. You will find Bread of Life and Living Water enough to fill you to overflowing."* Strength flooded my soul. I said yes and began.

Then a remarkable thing happened. Rather than dreading each day without food, I found the opposite to be true. Hope, confidence and passion began to replace my previous fear and exhaustion. I looked forward to each day's song from Father so much so that I actually found it difficult to get to sleep, such was the anticipation of what God was going to do the next day! Of course, I had moments of fighting through the mental battles that come with fasting, but thanks to the wisdom and nourishments in this book, I progressed into the fast as an adventure with God, slowly leading to a renewed mind, refreshed body, invigorated soul, and deeper faith. Dean's words and insight to Psalm 40 and Isaiah 40 led me to places of creativity and passion for Jesus that my soul craved. His encouragements can actually be heard in each of the songs I received during my fast. Believe it or not, I actually *enjoyed* the entire process! Food as an idol in my life was replaced by a proper focus on Jesus Christ as the Bread of Life.

Each day produced a new song of deliverance. My soul took flight. Even as I write this, I am anticipating a new fast. My friend, let this book and my songs inspire you. No one thinks they can manage an extended fast until you do one, then you discover the grace of God in such unique and personal ways! The benefits of fullness with God far outweigh a few days' emptiness in your belly. Renew your focus. Renew your focus on Christ, filled with Him above and beyond the cares of life. A brief "going without" during our time on earth brings about such a massive blessing that the momentary afflictions of the fast itself are erased by the eternal perspective you will gain. The simple riches in *Consumed* will become your faithful friend, full of encouragement, grace and sobriety to help you along the way. That's how it was for me.

I am so honored to make my songs available through the ebook version* of *Consumed*. As you read each day's Word and listen to the song, let it permeate your soul. While you may feel little from one day to the next, at the end of forty days, your life will be changed.

Be hungry. Be filled. Be consumed!

– Dennis Jernigan, worship leader
Founder, Shepherd's Heart Music

---

* Owners of the print edition receive a significant discount. See the last page.

"Resolved: that all men should
live for the glory of God.
Resolved second: that whether
others do or not, I will."

— Jonathan Edwards (1703-1758)
leader of the First Great Awakening

INTRODUCTION

*"Do not neglect the Forty Days;
it constitutes an imitation of Christ's way of life."*
— St. Ignatius of Antioch (35-108 A.D.)

YOU AND I, we've lost our way. Let us return to hunger.

We live in a *full* society, a full age. Compared to almost any other period in history, we lack seemingly for nothing, yet spiritually we are more dull than ever before. It requires no great insight to see that these two realities are directly connected, the former causing the latter. The Laodicean condition of the last days is the same as the rich man's dilemma when Jesus walked the earth. It's hard to want, much less penetrate and possess the kingdom of heaven when we're fat and happy on earth. Material prosperity and physical comfort effect a high toll on the human soul, slowly squeezing the *pneuma*, the spiritual breath of God out of us like a python suffocating its victim. While fullness of the Lord brings joy, other forms of fullness allow a scoffing, passive spirit to creep in, evidenced over time in our increasing disregard for the demands of true, spiritual life. Blindness, apathy, and a false sense of security are the long-term by-products. It's not a pretty picture, but it shakes down like this: when we are full of *stuff*, we tend to grow smug and complacent, unaware of our impoverished spiritual condition.

The irony, of course, is how we become blind even to our blindness. Deception is the hallmark of this miserable condition. Full of the pleasures of the age, we likely view our perpetual excess as the favor of the Lord. We're impressed with it. Should it breed comfort and detachment in our hearts, we do not grieve. We say, "I am rich, and have become wealthy, and have need of nothing." Yet the analysis of God is altogether different. In His eyes, we are "wretched and miserable and poor and blind and naked" (Rev. 3:17).

Get this right from the start: fullness is lukewarmness. Hunger is passion.

Fullness is dullness. Hunger is vigor.

Fullness is sleepy. Hunger is wide awake.

The connection to fasting is obvious, since one of the clearest evidences of our material prosperity is the buffet line. It takes neither a prophet nor a rocket scientist to recognize our love affair with food. Endless quantity. Endless variety. Food is a gift. But while it may be instrumental to sustain physical life, it also reveals important things about the state of our heart.

One of the most common, biblical, historical and effective means of addressing the problem of fullness is fasting. That's what this book is about. Fasting is uniquely effective at dealing with some of our most persistent, ingrained obstacles to wholehearted devotion: sensual cravings, lust, boredom, impatience, double-mindedness, pride, prayerlessness, lethargy, dullness. Fasting stirs up the full range of these vices and by exposing them, creates space for the Lord to answer with grace for: restraint, contentment, patience, focus, brokenness, intercession, vitality and tenderness.

From Day 1 to Day 40, this is meant to be a shared journey. On the one hand, it is the record of *my* journey. Though I have previously fasted periods of forty days, twenty days, with a few tens and threes thrown in for good measure, I would hardly consider myself an expert faster. Quite the opposite, lust for food has been one of the strongest, untamed compulsions of my life. While my high metabolism enabled me to justify my addiction, my portions have always been far too large to be reasonable. As I aged and my metabolism slowed, of course, the weight slowly came on. I became sluggish and disgusted with myself, not primarily because of the toll on my health and physique (though that was certainly a factor), but primarily because I knew I was the servant of every meal, and therefore at least one step removed from wholeheartedness to God.

Fasting has yet to become a lifestyle, but in the grace of God, my lifestyle is changing. It must, and none too soon. Discipline, restraint, vision, focus, passion, zeal and heightened sensitivity to the Spirit will be increasingly crucial in the final hours of human history. Thus, we simply can no longer afford to ignore the call to fast. This book will help you understand why, as well as serve as a guide for your own plunge into hunger. Fasting is no longer optional, it is mission critical. Over the course of forty days and forty nights, we'll dive in to the deep end.

Why forty? It is certainly not accidental. Forty is a taxing, consequential period — a number of mystical proportion in Scripture — rivaled only by 3 and 7 for significance. Consider a few examples (a more complete list is included in Appendix A):

1. During Noah's flood, it rained for 40 days and 40 nights
2. Noah waited another 40 days after the rain stopped before opening a window in the Ark.
3. Moses was before the Lord on Mt. Sinai 40 days when he first received the Ten Commandments. He spent a second 40 days of prayer and fasting on Mount Sinai to receive the Law a second time, after the original tablets were destroyed with the golden calf.
4. As penalty for their unbelief, the Israelites wandered through the wilderness for 40 years—one year for every day the original spies had been in the land. An entire generation of unbelief was forbidden access to the Promised Land. After 40 years were complete, Joshua led the Children of Israel across the Jordan River and conquered Jericho.

5. In the time of the Judges, after periods of repentance, the land was given rest 40 years at a time. (Judges 3:11, 5:31, 8:28)
6. Prior to beginning His public ministry, Jesus fasted 40 days in the wilderness.
7. Interestingly, the normal gestational period of a baby is 40 weeks. New life comes *after* 40.

The symbolism of the number is multilayered. On a basic level, it represents a long period of time as opposed to a brief period of time. Forty means delay. More importantly, the longer time has *purpose*. The waiting period is marked by need, struggle, testing, refinement. (In keeping with this, Jews developed a system of forty days spent in national and personal preparation before the most important holy day of their calendar, the Day of Atonement. This forty day window was a time of consecration and purification as the people trembled before the coming judgments of a holy God; more on that later in the fast). Deeper still, a third level of meaning becomes clear. Forty denotes a period of preparation for unique intervention or some other special action of the Lord; it is thus a time of grace. The test is refining on the one hand, but it can serve as a sort of validation on the other. The grace may serve to close one season and begin another. It is a time of change. The themes shape up thus: patience, endurance, purification, repentance, grace, rebirth. These threads will form your own story for the next six-weeks-minus-two.

Inspired by biblical precedent, we'll follow the example of Moses and Jesus, the pattern of Old Covenant and New, the testimony of law giver and grace giver. In so doing, we eliminate any argument of whether fasting is for *us*. Fasting was the tradition of the early church and countless notable saints throughout history.

Also in keeping with the 40 motif, it seems fitting to use two other notable 40's from scripture. Like a pair of glasses, Psalms 40 and Isaiah 40 will supply the interpretive lenses, the inspiration we need to see more clearly, that we might be more completely consumed with God. Don't expect an academic, linear series of teachings on fasting, but a loose progression of meaningful reflections. You hold a book of spiritual food, fuel for your journey. However, the following outline may be useful, as we explore:

1. The challenge to patiently persevere
2. Getting real with God
3. The need for humility and brokenness
4. Learning to hunger
5. Practicing denial and restraint
6. Developing a spirit of true repentance
7. Preparing for divine visitation
8. Understanding our reward
9. Growing deep in the majesty of God
10. Gaining new strength and vision

With empty bellies, we'll travel through twenty days of each chapter, one meditation per day, seeking a God who reveals Himself to weak, immature people—people who are far too full of the world, far too empty of Him—yet who desperately want transformation, a living experience with God, a more authentic faith. We will reflect on both the nature and process of fasting, as well as the rich personality of God, and how the latter uniquely uses the former to foster deep repentance and rebirth in our lives. So, no more Taco Bell, Pizza Hut, midnight snacks, ice cream sundaes . . . or buffets. We're cutting loose, getting free. We are going to embrace something lean, mean and hungry. Our prize: a spirit and soul scrubbed fresh for new encounters with Christ; a heart humbled by the pain of the process; a mind renewed with clean revelation from the Spirit and the Word.

Finally, this book is ideal for two categories of readers:

1. Anyone interested in the discipline of fasting, but not quite ready to take the plunge. If that's you, feel free to use this book as a

primer. Ultimately, however, I challenge you not just to read, but to join. The clear intention of this book is to stir you to make fasting a regular part of your journey with God, particularly a 40 day fast. Not yet, you say? No problem. Read anyway. Perhaps the Lord will add fuel to your fire with my observations.

2. The one who is ready to fast can use this as a guidebook and steady friend. I've provided room for you to journal your thoughts along the way, which I highly encourage as a record of this season in your life. Psalms 40 and Isaiah 40 will be marvelous companions for our journey together.

Incidentally, at the time of this writing, I am 40 years old.

It all seems perfectly aligned. Let's go.

REPENTANCE

*"Repent, for the Kingdom
of Heaven is at hand"*
— Jesus

DAY 1

I waited patiently for the Lord (Psa. 40:1)

CHANCES ARE good that you are waiting for something. Can you name it? Is it breakthrough, deliverance, healing, restoration? Perhaps you long for a more fervent heart for God, or joy in His presence. Deeper holiness. Quicker obedience. Breaking of addiction. Destruction of sin habits. Freedom. Global revival. All of it, right? But you have specific needs, too. What you need could be spiritual, emotional, physical, circumstantial, relational, financial. It's all part of this thing called life. The reason you are waiting is because *Needs* are not instantaneously matched with *Provision*. Lack is not instantly filled. Our questions are not instantly answered. Our pain is not immediately healed. Between the problem and the solution comes a period called Testing. The character meant to be produced by these tests is called Patience.

But I've waited so long it feels like forever, you say. And it probably does. You may feel like God is cold toward you and nothing will ever change.

To be human is to wait. It is a real form of suffering—no wonder we avoid it all cost! Yet patience is a sure sign of increasing spiritual maturity. One of the principal strategies of this age is to condition us to be fiercely intolerant of anything that requires us to wait. We defend this position even though Scripture confirms over and over that virtually all of God's promises took longer than anyone expected. Ask Noah, Abraham, Moses, David, Ezra, Nehemiah, Jeremiah, Daniel. Ask the Jews waiting for the Messiah.

Consider 400 years of Egyptian slavery, or 400 more in the "silent period" between the last of the prophets and the birth of Jesus.

> *"For the vision is yet for the appointed time; It hastens*
> *toward the goal and it will not fail. Though it tarries, wait*
> *for it; for it will certainly come, it will not delay."* (Hab. 2:3)

On our end, it feels like a *long* delay. But that's part of the problem. We don't have God's perspective. So here you are, ready to fast. Stuck and in need of breakthrough. Something violent and desperate has risen in your spirit. It's time to get a little crazy. That's good! But forty days and forty nights is a long journey. Patience is definitely needed. It doesn't matter how fierce and well-intentioned your early commitment is, you will quickly discover the limits of your resolve. Let me tell you in advance, by day 3, day 4, day 9, whatever it may be, you will start to tremble inside and think, *I don't know if I can do this. In fact, I'm sure I can't!*

And then you will think, *Well, if I'm going to fail, I might as well fail now.*

And then it will be over. But it doesn't have to be. Fasting, at heart, is an exercise of patience. It forces us to slow down, to feel the drag of time. When you are hungry, the day seems longer, not shorter. Embrace this. It is by design. You are on a journey into the patient nature of a God who has no regard for time. It is a paradox, in that you must embrace the suffering of fasting and learn patience by it, yet you must not yield the cry of your heart in defeat. Yearn for breakthrough, even when you do not see it. Do both: embrace and yearn. Wait and pray.

"If we hope for what we do not see, with perseverance we wait eagerly for it (Rom. 8:25).

Yes, there is a time to cry out, "Do not delay, oh God!" but it is not today. Your forty day fast will be forty days, not thirty, not fifteen, not five. Daniel did not receive the angelic visitation on the first day of his fast, but the last. There is a timeline. Submit to it.

There is warfare. Fight it. There is hunger. Feel it. As always, we are given a choice. We can wait patiently or impatiently. Either way, we wait. Use this time to build spiritual endurance. Many promises of God for you are contingent upon you building your patience muscles. It's just the way He works.

"For you have need of endurance, so that when you have done the will of God, you may receive what was promised" (Heb. 10:36). Like David in Psalm 40, let us start our forty waiting *patiently* for the Lord.

FAITH TIP

✓ As much as possible, minimize nonessential obligations. Carve out time wherever you can. Be deliberate to structure your forty days and forty nights with large swathes of time consecrated to the Lord.

VOICES OF WISDOM

✤ "First, let (fasting) be done unto the Lord with our eye singly fixed on Him. Let our intention herein be this, and this alone, to glorify our Father which is in heaven."

— **John Wesley (1703-1791)**

HEALTH SMART

✦ It is critical that you consult with your doctor about any modifications your particular health situation may impose upon your fast. *Don't fast* if you are pregnant or have an eating disorder.

REFLECTIONS

_____

_____

_____

_____

_____

DAY 2

He inclined to me, and heard my cry (Psa. 40:1)

HOW DO WE calculate the impact of this truth, that *God hears us*? Consider. From the splendor of His heavenly realm, would God-Beyond-Imagination be any less perfect if He had removed Himself entirely from our affairs? No. In His detachment, He would still be blameless, faultless, justified, ever perfect. After all, He gave life, moral law and dignity to man. What more do we expect from Him? Yet He drew near, of His own volition. He chose a people, invested Himself in our history. He guided, protected, delivered, corrected. To us, for us, He became Immanuel. He sent the Holy Spirit to take up residence in our human frame. God-Beyond-Imagination...

Inside you. Held within your mortal frame. Staggering!

Part and parcel of the revelation of His intimate concern for our lives is that when we cry out, He hears us. Be assured of being heard. You are noticed by God. Not in some passive way, not with bothered detachment. David says He *inclines* Himself toward us. It is actually a quite tender image. He leans toward you.

A proper understanding of this truth means we bear a certain responsibility in our miracle relationship with a tenderhearted God. Since it is established that He hears us...*what will we say to Him*? That's our part. No games. No pretending. Time to get real. What do we need, what do we lack? What burdens do we carry for which there is no comfort or remedy? Where are we stuck, broken, lost, hopeless, failing, flailing or fearful? For *what* do we cry out?

When Bartimaeus, an obviously blind beggar, stood before Jesus, the Lord asked a question that is almost offensive in it's obviousness and simplicity.

"What do you want?" He asked.

And then He listened. Jesus was invested, not detached. This was Bartimaeus's moment, with God enfleshed before him, leaning toward his sightless eyes, ready to respond.

Isn't it obvious, Jesus? I'm blind! I need to see!

No, Bartimaeus, actually it's not always obvious what we want from God—least of all to ourselves. We intensely feel our many needs on a variety of levels, but not always with clarity. Translate this story to America's modern welfare state, full of personal entitlement, and it is conceivable that Bartimaeus might have asked for any number of things: 1) a better cane for walking; 2) a significant financial breakthrough so that he didn't have to spend so much time begging; 3) a guide to help him move between premium begging spots. If Jesus were not a healer, or if Bartimaeus only knew him as powerful, influential, prophetic and wise, he might desire any of the above, or something else altogether ... but not healing. Strange as it may seem, Bartimaeus may have enjoyed all the pity and attention his blindness afforded him. Sometimes we do that, right? We hate our chains, our weakness, our condition ... and yet we revel in it.

Furthermore, we often stay stuck in complaining mode. We grumble because we need, but we don't always turn that need into a specific petition for comfort, relief or healing. We just stew in it and grow resentful. Or we pity ourselves. Or we take on a martyr's complex. Or we detach from relationship. Or ... or ... or ...

Right here, at the beginning of your forty days, settle it. In your hunger, in your need, Jesus stands before you, leaning in. His eye is on you in a unique way during this time. How do I know? Because Matthew 6:18 says that the one who fasts has a "Father who sees."

Adam, in the garden with God after the Fall, was seen. And yet, he was asked a similarly probing, seemingly obvious question: *Adam, where are you?* God saw him. God knew. Yet he asked, because Adam needed to see, Adam needed to know.

Reader, here it is: where are you? What do you want? It's time to get real with God and yourself. Why are you fasting?

FAITH TIP

✓ When you can't spend time in focused prayer, create prayer moments wherever you are. Every day is full of time for prayer: waiting in traffic, in line at the grocery store, cleaning dishes, in the shower, etc. Take the moments you are given and make something of them.

VOICES OF WISDOM

❖ "Prayer is not overcoming God's reluctance, but laying hold of His willingness."

— **Martin Luther (1483-1546)**

❖ "Nourish prayer by fasting."

— **Tertulian (c.a. 200 A.D.)**

REFLECTIONS

_____

_____

_____

_____

_____

_____

_____

_____

_____

_____

DAY 3

He brought me up out of the pit of destruction
(Psa. 40:2)

WE FAST FOR personal repentance. We fast for national revival. We fast for breakthrough, for intimate communion. We fast for discipline. We fast because we are trapped in a pit of destruction, literal destruction, and only God can deliver us.

The good news? Not only does God listen to our prayer, He acts upon it.

The good news? Not only does God listen to our prayer, He acts upon it. He responds to our need when we cry out for Him. Be assured, desperation is worth it. The pressure that brought you to this place has purpose. Get comfortable with pressure. It is good to be driven to the Lord. Become more desperate, not less. Yes, we must wait in patience. Yes, we must actually vocalize our need. But then He acts. And when God moves on your behalf, when the heavens part, the testimony of Jesus is established with new depth in your soul.

Isaiah, feeling the pressure, cried out, "Oh that You would rend the heavens! That You would come down!" (Isa. 64:1, NKJV)

During our fast, we ask Him to invade—oh please come down!—precisely that He might raise us up. This has always been the movement of God through redemptive history. It is His heart, His nature, His pleasure. He came down to Adam's fallen humanity to prophesy the salvation which would come through Eve and to provide a suitable covering for both their shame. He came down to Abram to declare the nearness of the promise which he and Sarai had circumvented with Ishmael. In spite of their old age, after God came down, Isaac was born a year later. He came down to Sinai to elevate a mass of slaves into a nation of conquerors, empowered by the knowledge of the laws of God to triumph in the new land.

> *Now it shall be, if you will diligently obey the Lord*
> *your God,* being careful to do all His commandments...
> *The Lord will cause your enemies who rise up against you*
> *to be defeated before you; they shall come out against you*
> *one way and shall flee before you seven ways.* (Deut. 28:1, 7)

If the people would but heed the word of God, victory was assured once God came down.

In Bethlehem, in the flesh of a human baby, He lowered Himself to redeem and elevate our existence from earthly to heavenly. Every one of these are pressure moments. Adam, trapped in the guilt of sin, with no idea how to atone for himself. Abram, full of ridiculously big promises that all depended on a son he was powerless to produce. Moses, facing the challenge of leading a people contaminated by their long residency in occultic Egypt and cast down in their identity by generations spent in servitude. The pressure squeezes us. It seems there is no way out. And it's true. Our destruction is assured. We're in a pit, often of our own making. We can't escape.

Until God invades.

When He comes down, everything changes. Isn't that worthy waiting, crying out for? Isn't it worth forty days?

HEALTH SMART

✦ Stay hydrated. Drink 6-8 full glasses of water a day. Purified water is even better.

VOICES OF WISDOM

❖ The secret formula of the saints: When I am in the cellar of affliction, I look for the Lord's choicest wines.

— Samuel Rutherford (1600-1661)

REFLECTIONS

_____

_____

_____

_____

_____

_____

_____

_____

_____

_____

_____

_____

_____

_____

_____

_____

_____

_____

_____

DAY 4

He set my feet upon a rock making my footsteps firm
(Psa. 40:2)

SHARP, ACTIVE HUNGER pains typically fade by day 3 or day 4. From then on, in a sense, it's all a mind game. Until now, your hunger pains have probably been rather sharp. If they haven't already, these will drop off significantly today, tomorrow at the latest.

Yet today, in your weakness, He wants to make your footsteps firm. This is the movement: we feel pressure, we need breakthrough, we wait patiently for His deliverance, we cry out our need . . . and then He comes down. He lifts us. In lifting, He moves us from uncertainty to certainty. He gives us firm footing. His salvation settles our soul. The wild fluctuations of emotional impulses that have dominated us become rooted in something more permanent. We find our place. We take our stand. We gain new perspective.

If you haven't noticed already, let me make the observation that your body has a clock. It *knows* when breakfast, lunch and dinner are due and it commands you to honor it with food. Your flesh has a will, a fact the Bible makes plain from cover to cover. Have you received Christ? Good, but remember, "We too all formerly lived in the lusts of our flesh, indulging the desires of the flesh and of the mind" (Eph. 2:3).

Your cellular structure has a natural process ordained by God that requires food to survive. God designed the body for food and food for the body. Before the Fall, He made the trees of the

Garden "pleasing to the sight and good for food" (Gen. 2:9). And again, in Genesis 9:3, God told Noah, "Every moving thing that is alive shall be food for you; I give all to you, as I gave the green plant."

Obviously, food is not evil, but our need for it does represent a will imposed upon us.

Obviously then food is not inherently evil, but the way our body depends on it does represent a will imposed upon us. In our brokenness, this physical will is co-opted by soulish impulses where sin struggles for mastery over us. According to sound Pauline doctrine, when the apostle refers to lusts and "carnal" desires of "the flesh" or the "old self" in Romans, Galatians and Ephesians, he is not speaking of your hunger for food, per se, but of the broken God-Receiver within that formerly caused us to turn to any source other than the Living Christ to fill our needs and satisfy our souls. If you can forgive a rather crude example, we're like an AM radio station that is constantly scanning crackling, static-filled airwaves for the next cool song, while God is waiting with a clear fixed signal on satellite. Not only are we searching for the wrong things, we're searching in the wrong way. In this sense, even good, natural physical desires (yes, like eating) can become corrupted instruments of our soul.

Your flesh wants you to serve it, and thereby become its slave. In America, excess is a cultural value, including savory pleasures. Is food wrong? Absolutely not! Yet it does represent control. The "flesh" of your soul will use your hunger to keep you enslaved, scanning every frequency, meal to meal, looking for satisfaction, never finding God.

He wants to establish something new in you. He wants to make a new kind of life firm under your feet. As you break free, hold fast to the Lord.

HEALTH SMART

+ During an extended fast, you may feel shaky or weak at different points of the day. Blood sugar issues vary from person to person and will likely be in flux until your body finds a new equilibrium. This can be uncomfortable, but is rarely serious. If needed, consider taking a teaspoon of peanut butter (or even better, raw almond or sunflower butter). The extra protein will help.

VOICES OF WISDOM

❖ "I often observe in fasting participants that . . . concentration seems to improve, creative thinking expands, depression lifts, insomnia stops, anxieties fade, the mind becomes more tranquil, and a natural joy begins to appear. It is my hypothesis that when the physical toxins are cleared from the brain cells, mind-brain function automatically and significantly improves, and spiritual capacities expand."

— **Gabriel Cousens, M.D.**

REFLECTIONS

DAY 5

He put a new song in my mouth, a song of praise
(Psa. 40:3)

ARE YOU FEELING strong today? Weak? Iffy?

Sometimes when you are weak, the only remedy is worship. For five days now, you have pressed into voluntary emptiness. Why have you done this? I'll tell you. You want to be filled with something else. You perceive the pleasures of this world are fading. The pleasures of sin pass away as soon as they are felt, leaving you more empty than you started. They have no eternal substance, no power to endure. Why build our life upon such flimsy materials? Together, we reject "worries and riches and pleasures of this life" (Luke 8:14) which choke out the seed of God within. We want good soil, that from the good seed of the Word planted in our hearts, we might bear good fruit.

John the Beloved tells us that we have been appointed to bear "fruit (that) would *remain*" (John 15:16). Eternal, enduring God-life within. Not the puff and pablum and cereal fillers of our modern diet, whether at the buffet line, the movie theater or in vain religious activities. The answer is not to counteract self and flesh with duty and obligation. We want a lifestyle of passion, joyful obedience and a true knowledge of God. It takes a cutting away, an act of circumcision. We choose not be full, than we might know our need. This is foolishness to the world. Even more when we turn our lack into praise.

In the grace of God, when we feel ourselves weakening, we turn to praise. We respond not with complaint or self-focus, but melodies of thanksgiving. There is a new song the Lord wants to give you—something fresh. It has the power to invigorate and inspire your own spirit even as you offer it to Him. This is not a song of lamentation for what you do not have, the meal you cannot eat. This new song emerges from the new thing you glimpse Him doing, even if your glimpse is only by faith. You see dimly, your belly groans, and you glance away to the hunger or some other distraction, because the promise seems so dim. No, keep looking! Even though there is pain in your stomach, you are beginning to feel the thrill of mastering your flesh by the power of the Holy Spirit, rather than serving it all day long, a slave, dawn to dusk.

That alone is cause for praise! Though we approach our mission with sobriety, the paradox of joy in this melody is that it emerges *from our emptiness.* On your low days, use worship to turn the tables. It is day 5. If you feel weak or discouraged, if your resolve has grown thin, remember that God is most near to the humble. He sees the small, feeble yes in your heart towards Him; it stirs up fierce, divine pleasure. Turn lack into praise and it will become a brightness in your spirit.

> *"Therefore the Lord longs to be gracious to you ... For though the Lord is exalted, yet He regards the lowly ... Draw near with confidence ... find grace to help in time of need ... power is perfected in weakness ... you have ravished My heart ... I have chosen and not rejected you"* (Isa. 30:18; Psa. 138:6; Heb. 4:16; 2 Cor. 12:9; Song 4:9; Isa. 41:9).

Rest in this: He is more involved in this process than you are. He is establishing something new, but it will take time. When you are weak, it is important to find praise and offer it. Make a routine of praise in the midst of your hunger. Find what He is doing inside and say yes, then exalt Him for it. Listen carefully, by faith. We are so used to loud noises. Fasting is meant to quiet us enough to hear the One for whom our soul longs.

What do you glimpse Him doing? Now sing it back to Him.

FAITH TIP

✓ Spend time today thanking God for His faithful guidance and involvement in your life.

HEALTH SMART

✦ Be practical. Don't cloister yourself away. Add fresh air and sunshine whenever possible. Thirty minutes of morning sun is ideal.

VOICES OF WISDOM

❖ "Be on your guard when you begin to mortify your body by abstinence and fasting—lest you imagine yourself to be perfect and a saint—for perfection does not consist in this virtue. It is only a help, a disposition, a means, though a fitting one, for the attainment of true perfection."

— St. Jerome (340-420 A.D.)

REFLECTIONS

_____

_____

_____

_____

_____

_____

_____

_____

_____

_____

_____

DAY 6

Many will see and fear, and will trust in the Lord.
(Psa. 40:3)

THE CRAVINGS AND temptations of our flesh are a miry, seemingly bottomless pit. We are easily trapped. It's hard to escape lusts that occur transparently in our brain as part of the normal routine of physical existence. Reasonable desires influence our thoughts, our time and buying habits nearly *carte blanche*. We accept them as normative precisely because they are! The problem is that they still tend to go unchallenged even when they exceed the parameters of what is healthy and godly.

Make no mistake, food is not explicitly evil. That is not the message of a fast. Eating disorders of extreme denial are demonic in nature, and severe monastic asceticism misses the point. We are setting our hearts to find God, to tenderize our spirit, not to punish the body or earn favor.

Sustenance was necessary prior to the Fall. *"God said, 'Behold, I have given you every plant yielding seed that is on the surface of the earth, and every tree which has fruit...it shall be food for you'"* (Gen. 1:29)

Adam and Eve feasted in the Garden before they sinned. But the Tree of the Knowledge of Good and Evil was also food! Forbidden food. In a sense you could say Satan used *excess food* to lead them to destruction, as the fruit of that tree went beyond what they were permitted. Even so, the desire for food was not wrong, only that particular meal. *It was more than was good for them.*

We have our pits as David had his. In Psalm 40, he begins by mourning the pit he has fallen into. When God finally raised him up, David recognized a higher purpose at work. Salvation was not for David alone. Many would take note, many would marvel at God. Many would decide from the example of David's life that God's leadership could be trusted.

"Many will see and fear and trust in the Lord."

This, too, is part of your journey. What God intends to reveal through your life is not only for your good, but for the fame of His name, the advance of His kingdom. The message of fasting is not that food is explicitly evil, but that too much is an impediment to deeper life. God desires to bring revelation through moderation to our spiritually starved culture. With supermarkets sagging under the weight of excess—not one variety of mac 'n' cheese, but ten! Whoppers and Big Macs dueling for loyalty! Every meal a feast of seconds and *thirds!*—your forty days of quiet, determined restraint may become the most shocking, unexpected, gracious invitation for others to follow the way of Christ.

In our culture of excess, your forty days may become a counterculture invitation for others to follow the way of Christ.

Others will take note. They will wonder. *C'mon, what's the big deal?* Many will experience conviction. You will be an enigma to them. Some may tease, maybe even mock—believers and unbelievers alike. *Radical,* they'll say. *Legalist.*

But some will begin to question the pit of excess we have all fallen into. Some of those, perhaps for the first time, will take up the cry in their own hearts: *Jesus above all other gods!* The pleasures of the world will begin to fade in their own affections.

They will begin to hunger.

HEALTH SMART

✓ It's important that you listen to your body, but don't overreact. Fasting for a long time is challenging. Your body is unaccustomed. It will feel strange from time to time. Most of the time, this is a good thing. Years of built up toxins are being released and eliminated. Be wise, but also don't panic.

VOICES OF WISDOM

❖ "When we finish a fast, we cool into tempered Christians strong with self-control. The dross and cinders of our lustful cravings are skimmed off. Fasting produces a work of art—the tempered, selfless Christian—that can be created through no other process of refinement.

— Lee Bueno

REFLECTIONS

_____

_____

_____

_____

_____

_____

_____

_____

_____

_____

_____

_____

_____

_____

_____

DAY 7

How blessed is the man who has made the Lord his trust
(Psa. 40:4)

TODAY IS YOUR fasting sabbath, the seventh day, which is the day of rest. If you are like me, somewhere along here a terrifying thought has probably gripped you: *Oh no, I've barely begun. I've got so long to go!*

You feel the intensity of this because you *want* to finish. How will you make it? You may even feel a sense of panic. What have I gotten myself into? But how can I quit? I'll be a failure. But how will I make it all the way? I can't! I *must*, but I can't!

Wait, slow down. Take a deep breath. Rise out of your belly and be gripped by the Spirit. Who are you trusting? Was forty days *ever* possible in your own strength? Take heart. You are well out of the starting gate. You're committed. Well done! Since more road lies ahead of you than behind, now is a good time to re-center.

"He who began a good work in you will perfect it unto the day of Christ Jesus" (Phil. 1:6)

To be established in a discipline like fasting requires our cooperation with the Spirit in developing the fruit of self-control, yet the prevailing power at work is the grace of God. It is "Him who is able to keep you from stumbling, and to make you stand" (Jude 24).

One of the benefits of fasting is that it lowers our spiritual center of gravity. By this I mean that the nature of persistently denying the flesh forces our personal supply lines to reroute from the outer man to the inner man. We gain new perspective externally, and peace internally, as we become less dependent on superficial needs. Fasting digs deep the inner wells of God. Reliable sensory experiences diminish. For example, most of us are used to three meals a day as reliable stimulation for our outer man. But no more. The things you used to trust to get you through the day can no longer be trusted: the hearty breakfast, the energy drink, the double latte, the Diet Dr. Pepper, the date night at your favorite restaurant with your spouse, the stolen little "chocolate moments."

The props are gone. You are left with you and a keen, unforgiving, unrelenting sensation of dissatisfaction, because your primary drives are being denied. It's aggravating. But it doesn't go away. And yet you desperately want to stay the course.

You have one answer, one hope.

As often as you think of food, turn to Him. Let Him become your food.

Trust in the Lord. As often as you think of food, turn to Him. Let Him become your food. Jesus said, "I am the bread of life. I am living water." (John 6:48, 4:10). As the living Word, He is sweeter than honey (Psa. 119:103). Jesus said, "Truly, truly, I say to you, unless you eat the flesh of the Son of Man and drink His blood, you have no life in yourselves . . . for My flesh is true food, and My blood is true drink" (John 6:53, 55).

As often as your emotions fluctuate or a pang of hunger stabs your belly, turn to Him. Lean on Him for strength. Feed on Christ. Feed on His Spirit. Cling to the hope of what He is doing inside you, unseen at present, but no less real. *Believe.*

Make the Lord your trust. You are on Day 7. Keep going!

FAITH TIP

✓ Don't presume upon the grace of God. *Ask* Him to supply the strength and resolve you need to complete this journey. The point of your fast is to fellowship with God. Turn thoughts and needs into conversations. Make a habit at the end of each day to ask Him for fresh grace for the next day.

VOICES OF WISDOM

❖ "A discipline won't bring you closer to God. Only God can bring you closer to Himself. What the discipline is meant to do is to help you get yourself, your ego, out of the way so you are open to His grace."

— James Kushiner

REFLECTIONS

_____

_____

_____

_____

_____

_____

_____

_____

_____

_____

_____

_____

_____

_____

_____

_____

DAY 8

Many, O Lord my God, are the wonders which Thou hast done and Thy thoughts toward us (Psa. 40:5)

TODAY, CHOOSE TO reflect on the goodness of God and His testimony in your life. Along the way, let's also connect some dots. During our first week together, we've been plowing our fallow soil in hopes of producing a more fruitful, heartfelt repentance. Of course, the spirit of repentance should infuse every moment of a fast. This means that as we take inventory of our lives, one of the first things we must decline (along with food) is our right to make excuses. No more shall we defend ourselves against the Holy Spirit's voice! A fast is holy reckoning. However painful it might feel, total transparency is a gift, because if we can admit our poverty, our great need of God, then the fast is destined to becomes a feast. In our hunger, we are consumed with love, by Love. This is good.

Facts are facts. We are easily *diluted*, spending our strength upon this and that, filled with too much clutter to maintain clarity, focus or impact in our service to the King. This is worthy of great sorrow, even though we may be too dull to know it. Fasting mercifully strips away these self-illusions until we find our voice to repent again. But true repentance is not gnashing our teeth in guilt and shame. It is responding to the grace by which the Holy Spirit changes us.

The last thing we want is token repentance. Let it cut *deep* and *true*. For this very reason, it would be most unfortunate to waste all your time dawdling and mewling over your great and terrible guilt. He knows! It's paid. Rather, it is the kindness of God that leads us to the turning ('Repentance': to change) we seek (Rom. 2:4).

Drawing upon today's verse, we steer our thoughts away from hunger to meditate more fully on the many kindnesses of God. We'll look at him through a supernatural lens tomorrow. For today, natural wonders of God abound . . .

Lightning in the storm.
Mother nursing her child. *Lion roaring.*
Man and woman, together.
Brother forgiving brother.
Courage on the battlefield.
Supernovas. Black holes.
Billions of stars. And galaxies
Dandelions in the wind.
Tenderness of a kiss. Poetry at dawn.
Laughter. Joy.
Hope.
Sacrifice to save a friend.

In these wonders, we glimpse the character of the Creator. Or as *The Message* translates it, "The world's a huge stockpile of God-wonders and God-thoughts." The stockpile may be "natural," but the wonders are no less staggering and beautiful in their simplicity, no less breathtaking and magical in their impact. They are like bonuses: you get to be alive *and* enjoy those things. Feast on them today, "filling your minds and meditating on things true, noble, reputable, authentic, compelling, gracious" (Phil. 4:8, MSG).

Let wonder whisper God to you. Deepen your appreciation for what you have been given: life, breath, and a mind capable of recognizing divine codes woven into the mundane. But wait . . . there's more!

He thinks about us. Go read today's verse again. It's a stunner. God . . . thinks . . . about *you.*

FAITH TIP

✓ To truly approach God in the way He desires, we must believe that He is a rewarder of those who diligently seek Him (Heb. 11:6). This may seem presumptuous, but it is vitally necessary. Are you persevering through this fast in the belief that God sees and knows your heart, that He loves you, that He has good things planned for your life? Meditate on the reward of God today and thank Him for it.

VOICES OF WISDOM

❖ "If a person makes fasting part of her or his life . . . By taking a long fast or two, and then fasting one day a week, s/he'll gradually find a growing peace and personal integration. America badly needs to go on a diet. It should do something drastic about excessive, unattractive, life-threatening fat. It should get rid of it in the quickest possible way, and this is by fasting."

— Allan Cott, M.D.

REFLECTIONS

_____

_____

_____

_____

_____

_____

_____

_____

DAY 9

There is none to compare with Thee (Psa. 40:5)

TODAY HAS BEEN a day of lightness for me. I feel healthy in a way I have not felt in many, many years. You will have days like today. After your body makes the initial adjustment to negligible calorie intake, it has a fair bit more energy (from fat stores, with no digestion tax) to put towards some basic housecleaning. As the body gets cleaner and lighter, you will reach a tipping point of general wellness that may surprise you with its lean, effervescent quality. Hunger may persist in factual terms, yet food will strangely matter less. The pressure becomes mental, not so much physical. You may still miss the sensation of eating, but your hunger is more of a mental habit than a physical need. Less truly becomes more. With excess slowly flushing from your system, you will begin to experience an alertness and general sense of wholeness unlike anything you've felt in a long while.

Mystery of mysteries, your body. We don't treat it very well. Paul majestically called it a temple, the very residence of God. A mystery beyond compare . . . save one.

"There is *none* to compare with *Thee*," David declared. Right in the midst of his trial, he was struck by the unfathomable splendor of God.

Let us now join David in considering the matchless qualities of God. Many could be contemplated, but for today we'll focus on the most fundamental essence of God: holiness. In modern parlance, 'holy' has become synonymous with 'pure', and by that we mean God is sinless, perfect, infallible, untemptably good (to the highest degree) beyond any capacity for evil. Pure, like distilled water. We may be dirty water, but He is unmixed. This application is completely true, but also secondary.

God is sinless and perfect, but holiness is more than simply perfect purity. Primarily, holy means God is *Other.*

Holiness is more than perfect purity. Primarily, holy means God is *Other.*

He is other than me, other than you. Uncreated, eternal, invisible, inconceivable. God is beyond and outside comprehension, beyond and outside logic. "How unsearchable are His judgments and unfathomable His ways!" (Rom. 11:33). You can't search long enough or deep enough to figure Him out. There is no bottom and no ceiling to God. He just keeps going. Limitless.

What does that even mean? Every time you see verses referencing the infinite nature of God or the highness of His ways, you are seeing the exalted language of holiness. If that's not helpful enough, another roughly equivalent, equally brilliant word is transcendence. Transcendence is the quality or act of *transcending.* Simply put, God is beyond, above, and different from every created thing.

What can you imagine? What do you know? He transcends it.

As a result of this indissoluble quality of God, man has a real dilemma. How can we possibly know something that is by definition unknowable? We can't! God must self-disclose or we would forever be trapped in endless, infantile speculations—the idea factories of our thoroughly non-transcendent minds. So though we don't deserve it, in love God bends low. He risks and reaches out. He tells us Who He is.

If it were not for this fact, God would remain a hopeless mystery, far removed from our lives. Man could be a seeker, but never a finder. There would be no concrete answers, and thus, no hope. The burden would rest entirely on man to find God, though it would remain impossible to do so. Any form of salvation we could glean would be entirely due to our own efforts, and all of them would fail.

Because God is transcendent, He *came* to us. This would not have been our plan, because weakness and humility is not our inclination. But He is not like us.

Yet precisely because God is transcendent and holy, because He is above, beyond, different—*He came to us*. This would not have been our plan, because weakness and humility is not our inclination. But He is not like us. In His eternal meekness, He spoke. Prophets declared him. Law revealed Him. Then, in the fullness of time, God sent forth His son, born of a woman. As one of us, yet *other* than us—sinless, perfect, pure—Jesus revealed God that we might at last come to know the Father through Him.

No, no, all other gods fail. There is *none* to compare with our God. He is beautiful beyond compare. To know this is to be undone. When we see Him, we join with the host of heaven and cry one word: "Holy!"

HEALTH SMART

✦ Light to medium walking is a good idea, but on a forty day juice or water fast, heavy exercise is not advised. Intense cardiovascular events such as jogging and weightlifting / muscle building exercises will be counter-productive. These should be suspended until the fast is safely over.

VOICES OF WISDOM

❖ "Fasting and natural diet, though essentially unknown as a therapy, should be the first treatment when someone discovers that he or she has a medical problem. There are hundreds of journal articles in the medical literature documenting the value of fasting in improving the function of the entire body, including the brain. The time may come when not offering this substantially more effective nutritional approach will be considered malpractice."

— **Joel Fuhrman, M.D.**

REFLECTIONS

_____

_____

_____

_____

_____

_____

_____

_____

_____

_____

_____

_____

_____

DAY 10

Sacrifice and meal offering Thou hast not desired;
My ears Thou hast opened (Psa. 40:6)

MANY ASSUME THE point of fasting is to develop greater hunger for God. The answer to this, of course, is yes. And yet . . . no. I believe the greater mission of a fast turns such straightforward logic on its head. Fasting is not a precise equation, but a deep, wrenching process. Just as you can't understand the appeal of a mystery book if you only read the first and last chapter, you cannot understand the spiritual hunger a fast is meant to produce if you skip too quickly to the desired outcome—spiritual hunger and connection with God—assuming a simple cause and effect process, like pulling levers and shifting gears on a machine.

We are *sensory* creatures. Our five senses represent a God-ordained system of interaction with a material world. Obviously, smell, sight, touch and taste are all part of eating. Even *hearing* gets in on the fun (the sizzle of a steak, the slosh of cold orange juice in a glass)! It's all good. Boy, is it ever good! "Food is for the stomach and the stomach is for food" (Rom. 6:13).

In contrast, *sensuality* is healthy sensory experience taken to excess. "For the time already past is sufficient for you to have carried out the desire of the Gentiles, *having pursued a course of sensuality,* lusts, drunkenness, carousals, drinking parties and abominable idolatries" (1 Pet. 4:3).

When I fast, what I am confronted most with is *not* my hunger for God, but my endless desire for nourishment. Food consumes my thoughts. *I want to eat.* I want satisfaction. I want the pleasure of a good meal. I want the smells, the textures, the colors, the delights. I am overtaken by sensory cravings. Daily, desire assaults me, so much that a brutal, humbling, almost shocking fact can no longer be denied: I am a man of flesh. In "normal life," in routine fullness, I am less cognizant of this fact, and it is no wonder. My next meal is at most a few hours away (with snacking, even less). The pain of hunger, of delayed satisfaction, of sensory deprivation, is greatly minimized. I don't have to face my deep, ulterior self. I can live on the surface, where I am stimulated, kept busy and full. Distracted.

However, when I fast, reality invades. The subtle grays of my foggy spiritual devotion are brought into bright contrast, high relief. My secret motivations, normally hidden even to me, become transparent. A terrifying picture emerges: life is all about *me. I* am hungry; *I* want to eat; *I* don't like self-denial and, really, *I* can't wait until it's over.

The plain, hard truth is that I desire fleshly things, not the things of the Spirit. It is shameful, but true. Fasting allows me to prove this to myself in a way my flesh cannot falsify or deny—it can't hide underneath my polite Christian exterior—because it's too busy lusting for and demanding appeasement. Far from any illusion of spiritual greatness, in the weakness of a fast I realize I have no strength or focus for prayer. I have no discipline. I am temperamental and irritable because the comfort of my flesh has been disturbed. I have no comprehension of God. The landscape of my soul stretches bleakly before me, and I am permitted the gift of sorrow.

Though we do everything we can to avoid it, Ecclesiastes profoundly affirms that sorrow is a gift. "It is better to go to a house of mourning than to go to a house of feasting" (7:2). *The Message* renders verse 4, "Sages invest themselves in hurt and grieving. Fools waste their lives in fun and games." Ouch and wow, both.

The discipline of fasting is a revelation of divine wisdom, precisely because it costs something; precisely because we can't afford the tab in our own strength.

FAITH TIP

✓ Don't plan for failure, but if in a sudden moment of weakness you grab a muffin or a banana or a ham sandwich, don't crash the whole program, either. Get back on your feet. Hit the delete button and begin again. Ask for mercy and strength . . . and more hunger. We are all weak vessels. God knows our frame, that we are but dust (Psa. 103:14). He is cheering you on. Get back on the horse.

VOICES OF WISDOM

✤ "People who think they are spiritually superior because they make a practice of . . . fasting or silence or frugality are entirely missing the point. The need for extensive practice of a given discipline is an indication of our weakness, not our strength. The disciplines we need to practice are precisely the ones we are not "good at" and hence do not enjoy."

— **Dallas Willard**

REFLECTIONS

_____

_____

_____

_____

_____

_____

_____

_____

_____

DAY 11

I delight to do Thy will, O my God;
Thy Law is within my heart
(Psa. 40:8)

BUILDING ON YESTERDAY'S theme, we see that fasting does not cause hunger for God so much as it serves to awaken the far more painful truth of how *little* we desire God at all. For the soul untrained by hunger, Jesus is a beautiful, divine option, adopted at our convenience, neglected at a whim. He is frequently Savior, thank you very much, but rarely Lord. In the scope of typical Christian commitment—witnessed daily in the lives of millions of good, sincere believers—God remains an abstraction, much like "heat" could be viewed as an abstraction of flame, when in reality our God is a Consuming Fire that burns, refines, transforms and does not apologize for His plans to take over planet Earth. When we are full, the coming Judge and Bridegroom King is like some unvisited Ninth Wonder of the World in a faraway land. He is both amazing and uncompelling. He dazzles, but we feel no urgency. No fire and blood, nor thunder in the chest; no pain and heartbreak; no glory and beauty, nor living obsession. He is something much more tame: a map for life, a wise counselor, a restrained, beneficent presence. Take Him or leave Him, really. It's okay either way.

Do those words offend? I hope so!

Perhaps you will answer, "Wait, that's not how I love God! He means more to me than that." And of course He does. He *is* more than that. He is everything. That being said, in all sincerity, do this to prove it: fast 40 days and see if you still feel the same. Does He *really* mean everything to you? Can you continue to invite Christ, experience Him in the presentness of your life, with no other props, only joy? Or in the midst of the fast, do you find yourself thinking about everything *but* Him. Careful, it's a dangerous discovery. But it's good. Peter brashly made his claims of devotion to Jesus before the Cross, then in the hour of testing his heart was stripped bare and the truth was plain for all to see.

An ancient Lenten hymn says, "Let us use sparingly words, food and drink, sleep and amusements. May we be more alert in the custody of our senses."

Now more than ever, we need to know this truth: do we live and move and have our being in Him? For those who wish to press in to God in this hour, it's utterly necessary not to play games or kid ourselves with illusions of commitment and relationship we don't in fact possess. If we live in the comfort of thinking God is something to us that in reality He is not, we need to know it. Sooner, rather than later. In this hour of history, later is too late. We are living in the days of the Five Virgins. Now is not the time for procrastination with our oil. If our vessels are empty, now is the time to buy oil. An ancient Lenten hymn says, "Let us use sparingly words, food and drink, sleep and amusements. May we be more alert in the custody of our senses."

At the same time, do not let fasting become a source of pride, a modern day equivalent "meal offering." Do not let it be a sacrifice of food which misses the point so much that you miss God. He is looking for "truth in the innermost" (Psa. 51:6). It is to the poor in spirit that the Kingdom of Heaven is promised (Mat. 5:1).

Are you hearing what your fast is telling you? Has your ear been opened?

Turn David's statement into reflection: Do you delight to do His will? Is His law written in your heart? Be frank with yourself.

Those who fast are not the elite, but the least.

You see, those who fast are *not* the spiritually elite. They are not the great saints, but the least. In the midst of forty days and forty nights, your leastness is made clear. The breaking and shredding of pride, the revelation of self, are both critical, because if we allow our hunger for food to prick our heart, the obsessive nature of our cravings will eventually drive us to God in prayer. We will begin to cry out, "God, I thought I wanted you, but I don't. I am fasting because I thought I wanted you, but now I see the truth. *I don't want you nearly as much as I want food.* What a fool I am! What a wretch. Though I am utterly in need of you, I just want to eat. Please awaken my heart to know my need. I can't escape from my lies unless you become my Truth. I am blinded by the cravings of my flesh. Indeed, I am poor and needy. I am spiritually bankrupt. The greatest thirst of my life is You, and yet all I care about, day after day, is my belly. Change me, oh God! Deliver me! Transform me!"

Pray it. Today, we must choke on our emptiness. I cannot afford to be impressed with my eleven days, nor can you.

I must have Him. You must.

This is why we volunteer for emptiness.

To be filled.

FAITH TIP

✓ Pray in the spirit. Not just when you run out of words, but also to tenderize your heart and gain clarity beyond natural reasoning. Build yourself up in your most holy faith. Strengthen your inner man. Pray in the spirit. You can't do this on your own, and even if you could, you would not want to. The last thing your weakened flesh needs is a proudly strengthened human will to rescue it.

VOICES OF WISDOM

❖ "Jesus has many lovers of His kingdom of heaven, but he has few bearers of His Cross. Many desire His consolation, but few desire His tribulation. He finds many comrades in eating and drinking, but He finds few hands who will be with Him in His abstinence and fasting."

— **Thomas a Kempis (ca. 1380-1471)**

REFLECTIONS

_____

_____

_____

_____

_____

_____

_____

_____

_____

_____

_____

_____

DAY 12

I have not hidden Thy righteousness within my heart;
I have spoken of Thy faithfulness
(Psa. 40:9-10)

IN THE WISDOM of God there is a strategy to fasting, the full scope of which has been reserved for the end times church; that's you and me, by the way. If the various quotations I've included are meant to convey anything, it is that this wisdom is hardly some newfangled idea. It is an ancient lifeline for the spirit, a testing of the flesh. Even so, fasting's full application will only be realized in the context of the crisis coming to planet Earth. Before the Lord returns, fasting will be realized as a critical component of His final war plan. Just as Jesus fasted forty days before embarking on three-and-a-half years of the systematic destruction of Satan's dominion, so shall extended periods of fasting unleash the presence of God within His church in unprecedented measure in the days ahead. Globally synchronized solemn assemblies, lifestyle fasts and extended 20, 30 and 40 day fasts will become commonplace, as the church is transformed into an unstoppable wrecking ball against the kingdom of darkness.

Is there a link between fasting and establishing the presence of God within? When the disciples of John asked Jesus why His disciples did not fast as John's did, Jesus answered, "The attendants of the bridegroom cannot mourn as long as the bridegroom is with them, can they? But the days will come when the bridegroom is taken away from them, and then they will fast" (Mat. 9:15).

Surprisingly, this is the deep heart of the New Covenant fast: mourning. In His absence we mourn and hunger and thirst because nothing else satisfies like His presence. We either mourn because we realize it is true, and therefore we fast. Or we fast because we do not yet feel it as Jesus Himself declared we would. In repentance and obedience, we fast *until* we mourn. Fullness diminishes our internal awareness, but fasting reconnects us on a deep emotional level to the pain of His absence. You may wonder, how can that be true if we carry the Holy Spirit which Jesus sent, which is the Spirit *of Christ* (Rom. 8:9)? How can we mourn His absence? Well, how can you have letters, cards and tokens from the one you love—how can you talk to them on the phone—but if they are far away, your heart aches? It is lovesickness. The Holy Spirit is not resentful of our emotions for Jesus, He encourages them! In fact, that same Spirit joins with the Bride in the final hour, crying out, "Come!"

No more veil. No partial glimpses or unrequited longing. Visible, physical presence. The righteous rule of a righteous King.

As it pertains to us, the righteousness He imputes is not meant to be hidden, but translated into mighty exploits (Dan. 11:32), works of justice (Isa. 58:6-8, Mat. 25:34-36), and the global proclamation of the nearness of the Kingdom (Mat. 10:7-8; Mark 16:15-18). We are to shine brightly in the midst of increasing darkness, like a city on a hill (Mat. 5:14; Isa. 60:1-2). We are meant to be bold, faithful witnesses, trumpeting the clarion call of the gracious invitation of God to a world that rejects Him, and therefore us. Yet we press on. We bow our knee to no one but the Lord Jesus. Speaking of His own return, Jesus asked whether He would find faithfulness. David reminds us, that's *our* job.

"I have spoken of Thy faithfulness."

We don't hide it, we declare it. Fasting helps both to prepare the message within us, as well as to prepare us to bear the message with integrity and boldness. What is your confession of the Lord? Declare His faithfulness until He comes.

HEALTH SMART

✦ Consider a good quality herbal tea as part of the fluids you drink. A variety of "cleanser" formulations can be found at any reputable health food store. Prepare these plain and sip a cup or two a day in addition to the water you consume. Various combinations of herbs in the tea may include milk thistle, burdock root, chickory, uva ursi, cinnamon, clove, dandelion root, juniper berries, chaparral, red clover, poke root, sheep sorrel and others that will help strengthen the kidneys and liver as they cleanse the blood and renew your body.

VOICES OF WISDOM

❖ "With physical fasting and, even more so, with interior fasting, the Christian prepares himself to follow Christ and to be His faithful witness in every circumstance. Moreover, fasting helps us to understand better the difficulties and sufferings of so many of our brothers and sisters who are oppressed by hunger, severe poverty and war."

— **Pope John Paul II (1920-2005)**

REFLECTIONS

_____

_____

_____

_____

_____

_____

_____

_____

_____

DAY 13

Thy lovingkindness and Thy truth
will continually preserve me
(Psa. 40:11)

IT COULD BE SAID that in its simplest reduction, sin is confidence in the flesh. Rebellion? Yes. Selfishness? Yes. Pride? Check. An accusing, degraded view of God? You betcha. All of these are manifestations of trusting ourselves—our strength, wisdom, ability, insight, etc.—more than trusting the timing, kindness, leadership and provision of God.

- Eve believed a lie about God and found food more desirable than glory.
- Adam more flagrantly rebelled. He knew it was a lie and ate anyway.
- Moses, exhausted, did not turn to the Lord, but to his anger. He struck the rock when he should have spoken to it.
- David called for a census to prove the strength of his army, and the Lord's anger burned.
- Solomon, representing the pinnacle of human wisdom, turned to rampant polygamy and countless treaties with foreign nations to fortify his kingdom.
- Peter thumped his chest and boasted of his fidelity to Jesus only a few hours before shaming himself three times.

In every case, then and now, we stray from the Lord when we put confidence in the flesh. To do so is pride, rebellion, selfishness, foolishness . . . and therefore wickedness. It is the dilemma of human nature. "All of us have become like one who is unclean, and all our righteous deeds are like a filthy garment" (Isa. 64:6).

When we accept the loving call of God to be born of Spirit, His grace initiates a new existence. It is the fulfillment of the original privilege of humanity . . . to freely enjoy the beautiful transfer of His life into ours.

Born of Adam's seed, corruption is inevitable. However, when our eyes are opened, when we accept the loving call of God to be born a second time of Spirit, not flesh, we enter a covenant of grace by faith in the One Who called us. Our lives bathed in mercy. We begin a new kind of existence, breathing the air of heaven while bestriding earth. We begin to fulfill the original privilege of humanity, freely enjoying the beautiful transfer of His life into ours.

Yet all too often—almost universally I'd say—a subtle erosion occurs with surprising swiftness. The devastation to our soul is real. In striving for God, we begin to labor in our own strength again. We know better, but we do it anyway. Grace remains the solid theology of our salvation; not so much the sustainer of our daily lives. To the degree this occurs, the flesh rears its ugly head again, along with pride, selfishness, etc. Before long, our heart is full of inward boasting of such things as our dedication to God, our steady denial of sin, our spiritual gifts, our soul-winning, our blessing . . . yes, our fasting. Conversely, should we fail and fail again—should our lives be marked by everything but triumph—we equally fail the test of grace, just in the opposite direction. We become dejected, rejected, despairing, miserable creatures. Saved, but barely.

No, no beloved. In both cases, no. Whether we stand or fall, whether we fast or feast, we are the Lord's. His grace saves *and* sustains. His goodness draws *and* keeps us. His kindness comforts and heals at all times, in all seasons, in every condition of our soul. As we fast, we must flee self-striving and pride, but also self-contempt and defeatism.

"Whom have I in heaven but Thee? And besides Thee, I desire nothing on earth. *My flesh and my heart may fail,* but God is the strength of my heart . . . as for me, the nearness of God is my good" (Psa. 73:25-26, 28).

He draws near, not because we fast, but because He is good.

He draws near, not because we fast, but because He is good and He loves us.

"And so we know and rely on the love God has for us." (1 John 4:16, NIV). Or as *The Message* translates Psa. 40, "Your love and truth are all that keeps me together."

Today, believe. His lovingkindness and truth will continually preserve you.

HEALTH SMART

✦ Common side effects from an extended water or juice fast can include headaches, dry, cracked lips, dizziness, constipation (if adequate fluids are not consumed), heartburn, slightly blurred vision, skin rashes, coldness (due to blood sugar fluctuations and fat loss) and, of course, fatigue. Fuzzy, unfocused thinking can also occur. Generalized aches and pains might surface in various regions of the body, often where the body is working to restore itself. These admittedly unpleasant feelings may persists until your body "turns the corner" in cleansing itself, but are rarely serious. Usually, they are a good sign!

VOICES OF WISDOM

❖ "Throughout history, men have fasted with a wrong spirit as they sought to earn God's favor or man's approval. Some embrace extreme self-debasements to try to prove their dedication to Him or earn His favor. This is not what God is after. He delights in our pursuit to love Him and to believe His word. We do not fast to prove anything to God or to deserve His favor. We fast to position ourselves to receive freely from His grace and be preoccupied with Jesus and His will."

— **Mike Bickle**

REFLECTIONS

_____

_____

_____

_____

_____

_____

_____

_____

_____

DAY 14

For evils beyond number have surrounded me (Psa. 40:12)

HERE'S A NO BRAINER: life is hard. Have you ever felt like David? Outnumbered, outranked, outgunned. It's like that awful dream we all have when we're kids. You know the one. You're somewhere in public wearing nothing but your skivvies. Except the grown-up version adds a bull's eye to your rear end and drops you in a closed room full of rabid, storming bulls, with big long horns and fire in their eyes. As you run and scream and try to find the door (there is none), your only consolation is that the hungry lions and tigers also in the room will probably eat you first. Weird dream, huh?

Some days I wish it was just a dream.

Evils beyond number *have* surrounded me before. How about you? Not to mention countless discouragements, temptations and obstacles of every stripe.

Lest you think I refer to life as being merely challenging (like time management is challenging, or water polo), let us return to Scripture for understanding the terms of our struggle. "For our struggle is not against flesh and blood, but against the rulers, against the powers, against the world forces of this darkness, against the spiritual forces of wickedness in the heavenly places" (Eph. 6:12).

This is a bloody, no-holds-barred battle for mastery of the human race and planet Earth. The evils we face include addictions, strongholds and complex world systems energized by cruel demonic power. Brilliantly perverse strategies supervised by the highest ranking offspring of Hell are executed millions of times daily on unwitting human victims.

Yeah, you got a bull's eye.

This is part of the reason fasting must become a compelling practice; a necessary, vital habit more than a luxury. Darkness is and will continue to escalate in all manner of perversity. How do you plan to stand in faith in the days ahead? Jesus described these days as so severe that men would be "fainting from fear and the expectation of the things which are coming upon the world" (Luke 21:26). He said that "many will fall away" and "most people's love will grow cold," that it would be global cataclysm on a scale "such as has not occurred since the beginning of the world until now, nor ever shall" (Mat. 24:10, 12, 21).

He warned us. There will be a price for loving Him at the end of the age. Endurance will be required. Naming Jesus will cost something.

In that day, evils beyond number will continually surround us all.

"He who endures to the end . . . shall be saved" (vs. 13).

But how do you learn perseverance on that scale? You have to grow in it. "If you have run with footmen and they have tired you out, then how can you compete with horses?" (Jer. 12:5). The end of the age will be a horse race, not a foot race. Fasting is the ideal exercise to stretch your endurance muscles. Can you fast for one day or week? Good, try three! Have you fasted for five consecutive days? Excellent, now try ten. Then 20. Then 40. See?

Fasting is an utterly practical, useful discipline the Lord has given His Bride to help her prepare for the coming trials. However, the deeper exposure of your heart to the flaming love of God is the real key. When evils surround you, lean into the fire of God. Demons tremble before the holy, judging presence of the God from whom they have been cast away.

HEALTH SMART

✦ Fasting not only detoxifies the soul, it detoxifies the body. As a result, it is natural to experience a period of unusual body odor and unpleasant tastes, perhaps even a coating, on the tongue. These could vary from minor to foul, depending on your particular health profile and what your body is laboring to cleanse.

VOICES OF WISDOM

✤ "If a king wanted to take possession of his enemies' city, he would begin by cutting off the water and the food and so his enemies, dying of hunger, would submit to him. It is the same with the passions of the flesh: if a man goes about fasting and hungry, the enemies of his soul grow weak."

— Abba John the Dwarf
(Desert Father from the 4th century Egyptian wastelands)

REFLECTIONS

_____

_____

_____

_____

_____

_____

_____

_____

_____

_____

_____

_____

_____

_____

_____

DAY 15

My iniquities have overtaken me, so that I am not able to see.
They are more numerous than the hairs of my head;
and my heart has failed me. (Psa. 40:12)

WE KNOW IT all too well. We can recite it in our sleep: "All have sinned and fallen short of the glory of God" (Rom. 3:23).

We know it so well we have grown comfortable with it. When was the last time the knowledge of your great need of God *devastated* your heart? Has Romans 3:23 become a sort of status-quo claim for our lives, a verse we use to rationalize the allurements of sin, and in so doing actually fortify our minds against conviction by the Holy Spirit?

Well, I'm just a sinner. What do you expect?

No, you are a new creation in Christ! We have become pacifists to our own nature—the death of the old, the newness of the new—and the ongoing toll of our ignorance should stir something akin to grief-stricken violence. Really, who are we kidding? Our society is literally collapsing. Divorce and pornography rates are virtually identical between church and world. Millions of babies are killed every year, heinous acts of sex trafficking are skyrocketing, and the homosexual agenda has been pushed to the point that a Washington legislator recently advocated *the abolition of marriage!* Our moral barometer is in a tailspin, politicians are elected with full knowledge of their corruption, public policy is bought and sold, and yet we can't spend enough on Dish Network, McDonald's or that shiny new iPhone/

Honda/Macbook/Abercrombie/CD/Movie *ad nauseum* to stir ourselves to wakefulness, much less an appropriate sense of outrage. If there is a song playing while Rome burns, the Church is holding the fiddle.

Oh, we need revival! To become a people deeply marked by the virtue, wisdom, love and power of God! And if not . . . why? David took a look at his life and, in the midst of His confidence in the lovingkindness of God, *grieved* to see how far He had missed the mark. We are correct to rely on the extravagance of grace, but a true biblical understanding of God's kindness is meant to awaken full-throttled agreement with His leadership and direction of our lives, not a complacent, "Oh thank goodness, I'm covered." His kindness *leads us* somewhere even while it comforts and sustains along the way. It shepherds us toward desperation and heartbreak over all the ways we reject His leadership. The best repentance is the joyful, searing, shocking, total recognition of our need for Christ. *I* need Him, *you* need Him. We must behold Him! The desires of our old man were badly bent. We are prone to persist in their crookedness. Iniquities abound in our culture, but that is to be expected. What is troubling is how often the people of God are indistinguishable from the problem. Like David, we have lost our way. We can't see clearly. We choose poorly. We *sin*.

God save us.

Of course by His blood, He already has. There is no other means by which we are saved. Even so, disciples of Jesus commit to a never-ending progression of alignment to His will. This occurs in a variety of ways: prayer, the Word, worship, meditation, acts of justice. Most of all, we continually renew our minds to the lordship of Christ, His provision of righteousness, and our union with Him. But when we need a deeply personal revolution—when our cry takes on the urgency of David's—it is the grace of fasting to which God directs us in our battle against friendship with the world.

"Or do you not know that friendship with the world is hostility towards God?" (James 4:4)

When iniquities overtake you, when you glimpse your need for personal revolution, a *forty day* fast is most effective. You are on Day 15. Keep going.

FAITH TIP

✓ You will get distracted. Various realities of life will impose themselves on your day. All of a sudden, long delayed chores and tasks will come due. Part of the test of your forty days will be in time management and a certain dogged willingness to bounce back from the little setbacks. A thousand cuts can bleed your strength as surely as one fatal wound. Three words matter: focus, focus, focus.

VOICES OF WISDOM

❖ "Freely chosen detachment from the pleasure of food and other material goods helps the disciple of Christ to control the appetites of nature, weakened by original sin, whose negative effects impact the entire human person. Since all of us are weighed down by sin and its consequences, fasting is proposed to us as an instrument to restore friendship with God."

— **Pope Benedict XVI**

REFLECTIONS

_____

_____

_____

_____

_____

_____

_____

_____

DAY 16

Be pleased, O Lord, to deliver me.
Make haste, O Lord, to help me. (Psa. 40:13)

IF FASTING IS a unique grace, it is also warfare. God employs it like dynamite in the soul, to break loose the calcified chunks of our heart that no longer live before him but routinely gorge on the world's pleasures. If our soul is anemic, fasting is iron in the blood. If we are paralyzed, fasting is spinal surgery and muscular electrolysis. If we are blind, fasting is Lasik. We fast from anything and everything needed to shake ourselves awake: food, finances, use of time, words, energy, entertainment. We get violent. We become restless, urgent for deliverance.

"Make haste, O Lord, to help me!" we cry. We hear the echo of a chorus of saints down the corridors of history, joining us. We cannot save ourselves, but we can choose to become lean and fervent unto the day of our salvation. David gives us words to launch back towards the heavens.

God, do something!

And God does. He floods in, cleansing our souls, rejuvenating our sense, washing our conscience, tenderizing our spirit, empowering our character for godliness.

Again, forty days is a key number. It's not random. It's strategic. Remember, Moses and Jesus both fasted forty days.

Be strengthened in this: your forty *means* something.

We might glimpse more about forty through the lens of Jewish tradition. For centuries, Jews have intentionally transferred the understanding of a meaningful symbol (like forty) to other facets of daily and religious life, believing that patterns revealed in Scripture merit replication elsewhere, thus adding richness to their faith. For example, when a person becomes ritually impure, he undergoes a ritual bath called a *Mikveh*. The Talmud (a revered collection of ancient rabbinical discussions) declares that the Mikveh cleansing must be accomplished with forty measures of water; also that the person must be completely submersed. Once this is accomplished, the person leaves the Mikveh ritually pure. The pattern they follow comes from the revelation of Noah's flood, when the rain poured forty days and forty nights. Before the flood, the world was utterly corrupt. When the waters of the flood subsided, the world was purified of evil and given a fresh start. The wisdom of the rabbis is that if 40 units of water was an adequate measure for the cleansing of the earth, then forty waters of a Mikveh are sufficient for cleansing, as well.

Likewise, according to a great Jewish intellect called the Maharal (16th century Prague), forty contains the power to elevate a thing's spiritual state. The Hebrew children arrived at Sinai a nation of Egyptian slaves. After forty days of covenant revelation and Law given to Moses, they were ennobled beyond servitude to become the very nation of God on the earth. They were promised rulership. They were given a new identity, a code, cohesion as a people. The promise to Abraham, tested by the humiliations of Egypt, was now elevated and established at the base of the holy mountain. *But only after forty days.*

When you start to feel reckless, holy urges; when you gasp in your spirit for more of God and less of you; when you become discontent with your contentment, forty days have been prepared for you, too. You are on Day 16. Keep going.

FAITH TIP

✓ Make prayer lists. This is not legalism, but practical and wise. We all want to pray, but in the moment of prayer, we often draw a blank. Make lists for: Personal Breakthrough, Family Needs, National Sins, etc. These lists will focus your time and yield productive dialog with God.

VOICES OF WISDOM

❖ "There is nothing which so certifies the genuineness of a man's faith as his patience and his patient endurance, his keeping on steadily in spite of everything."

— **Martyn Lloyd-Jones (1899-1981)**

REFLECTIONS

_____

_____

_____

_____

_____

_____

_____

_____

_____

_____

_____

_____

_____

_____

_____

DAY 17

Let those be ashamed and humiliated
together who seek my life to destroy it;
let those be turned back and dishonored
who delight in my hurt. (Psa. 40:14)

AT THE TIME OF the writing of Psalm 40, David faced an onslaught of accusation from his enemies. The wrenching nature of this psalm arises from his feelings of entrapment and slander. The maliciousness of David's foes greatly tempted him to despair. Why are humans so prone to feelings of hopelessness?

Our enemy is not only inward in lust or external in the pleasures of the age, but also deeply spiritual. Satan "delights in your hurt" far more than did David's foes.

The reason is because we have an enemy beyond flesh and blood. Our enemy is not only inward (lusts of the flesh), and not only external (pleasures of the age), but also deeply spiritual. Every day, demonic forces align to afflict you with all manner of ungodliness. Satan "delights in your hurt" even more than did David's foes. As Jesus made clear, the evil one comes "to steal, kill and destroy" (John 10:10). In other words, like David, he "seeks (your) life to destroy it."

The vicious, relentless nature of Lucifer's hatred for humanity is so shocking, our normal reaction is to recoil—and to a certain degree, disbelieve. It's a form of coping and compensation. Since even sinful humans possess an instinct for compassion, we cannot easily reconcile or conceive of pure evil. Instead, we subconsciously recalibrate our image of the enemy, subtly reducing his true malevolence to comic hyperbole (the red devil with pitchfork and horns), as if Satan was really just a grumpy, bad-tempered prankster who doesn't like you and me very much.

It's a lie.

No, rather he is the second most powerful being in the universe, a dark, cruel spirit intent on bringing destruction, chaos, lawlessness and death anywhere he is permitted. He is the most brutal serial killer in history. He is an insane and wicked genius; totally depraved, totally corrupt, totally bloodthirsty. He is the most vile stalker, pervert and sexual predator. He is ancient in deception, cruel beyond fathoming, forever unrepentant, and powerful beyond your worst nightmares.

He is all of this in the most terrifying demonic form, master to millions of hateful servants who slavishly spread his evil across the planet. He has a blood grudge against God and, being both foolish and proud enough to think he can achieve his ultimate aim, is bent on nothing less than the total annihilation of humanity.

He wants to control history. He wants to control *you*.

If he can't, he wants to kill you.

Amazingly, in Christ, you have nothing to fear from him, but you do need to know:

1. He is real
2. He wants you destroyed; therefore,
3. You must learn to cry out to God

Until Christ returns and Satan is bound at last for a thousand years, the accuser of the brethren will relentlessly seek every opportunity to ruin and defile your life. He has developed successful strategies over multiple millennia of interaction with human beings, including: slandering God to you, slandering you to God, slandering you to yourself, boasting of you to yourself, boasting you against God, boasting you against your neighbor, slandering your neighbor to you, sowing dissension, feeding pride, corrupting desires, tempting with false rewards, turning freedom into bondage, unleashing curses on the unknowing, robbing blessings, breaking covenant, stealing health, inflicting disease, inflaming dark passions, inciting violence, hatred, strife and murder, and countless other sinister designs.

By the time you've gone to bed at the end of any given day, you've literally been through hell. The battle is serious. You need protection and grace. You need armor. You need truth. You need power and insight. You need courage.

You need God.

To paraphrase: "Let every enemy of my soul be turned back, oh God! Let all demonic assignments come to shame. Let them fail in every attempt to dislodge me from Your grace, Your love and Your plan for my life. Let the enemy fall into the very pit he's dug for me. Save me and deliver me! Vindicate me with such zeal that the enemy is not just defeated, he is humiliated."

Fasting, for good reason, is warfare. The battle is on your doorstep. Go to war.

FAITH TIP

✓ Satan does not respond casually to a heart set Christ. He will resist your forty days. He will busy your day, tempt your mind, attack your will, stir pride and lust. He will arrange difficulties to test you and make you return to the easy comforts of food. He will try to weaken your resolve. Ironically, you may find it easier to resist than ever, but stay alert.

VOICES OF WISDOM

❖ "Fasting cleanses the soul, raises the mind, subjects one's flesh to the spirit, renders the heart contrite and humble, scatters the clouds of concupiscence, quenches the fire of lust, and kindles the true light of chastity."

— St. Augustine (354-430)

REFLECTIONS

_____

_____

_____

_____

_____

_____

_____

_____

_____

_____

_____

_____

_____

_____

_____

DAY 18

Let all who seek Thee rejoice and be glad in Thee.
Let those who love Thy salvation say continually,
"The Lord be magnified!" (Psa. 40:16)

TODAY IS A DAY of praise. It is a day to focus on the Lord and serve His pleasure rather than your needs. Notice, you do not have to rejoice in your fast. Your circumstance may feel quite barren or discouraging. Thankfully, you are not commanded to rejoice in your circumstance, but to "be glad *in Thee.*"

Let's dig deeper into the purpose of fasted worship.

It has already been noted that when Israel journeyed into the wilderness, after spending 40 days at Mt. Sinai, their covenant with Yahweh was established. This is of primary importance, but it is really the mirror image, the flip-side of the command the Lord gave Moses, which he in turn repeatedly spoke to Pharaoh. This command helps us understand our own 40 day wilderness.

"GOD, the God of the Hebrews, sent me to you with this message: 'Release my people so that they can *worship me in the wilderness*'" (Exo. 7:16 MSG).

We come to Sinai, to the place of testing, revelation, covenant and grace, to learn to worship Yahweh. Here, his law is written upon our hearts in a new way. Here, we behold Him in a new way. We become low in our eyes; He becomes high. We respond in worship. The mountain may thunder or seem quiet, but one thing is certain. In this stretch of time, the idols of our heart will beg us for attention. We *will* give our time to something when we cannot give it to food, just as Israel gave it to a golden calf. What commands our affection? Those who love the salvation of God are challenged to have a *continual* God-centered response, "The Lord be magnified!"

But perhaps we can go a bit deeper, because many things occur simultaneously at the mountain of the Lord. In the overarching purposes of God, we know the Father is seeking those who will worship Him in spirit and in truth (John 4:23). Jesus, quoting Isaiah, pinpointed a common hindrance to this when he said we often honor the Lord with words of praise even though our hearts (behavior, thoughts, feelings) are far from him (Mark 7:6). If we want to worship in spirit and truth, our lives must be deeply pleasing to Him. We must harmonize with His melody, be godlike, rather than god-opposed. We don't want to play sour notes, sing off key or create competing musical phrases. And make no mistake, words of praise are simply not enough. We must *become* worship.

The way we treat others is just as much a part of worship as the way we treat God.

For this to happen, we must recognize the full scope of God's intention in transforming a nation of slaves into the people of God, for such are we. Any tendency toward revenge, injustice, or the darker sides of human passion must die and be reborn in the likeness of Christ.

Listen: the way we treat others is just as much a part of worship as the way we treat God.

Back to Sinai. Whenever a people group has been oppressed, as were the Hebrew slaves, a unique human dynamic is revealed: some people are weak, others are strong. Some are oppressed, others are oppressors. Likewise, history convincingly reveals that, given the chance, we're really all the same. We all love power, domination, control. The only difference between the two groups is a matter of timing, privilege and circumstance, but should the tides turn, the victims of today will most certainly become the taskmasters of tomorrow.

Something must change or nothing will change. And it must change *within*.

Newly delivered from the lash in Egypt, what might the Israelites have done with their newfound power and "blessed" status without their 40 days at the mountain of God? Moses eventually prophesied to them that they would be the head and not the tail if they kept the covenant of God. But how would the head behave? What kind of moral basis would inform their justice, their compassion? Fundamental to Sinai is a whole different view of reality, a new set of values, a totally different style of life. The groundwork was laid for how they would later be taught to treat the stranger, the oppressed. They were no longer slaves, they were children of God. They had to understand how God thinks. They had to see themselves differently in order to see others differently. The only way to break the chain was to become bonded to Yahweh.

Jesus was also tempted to sing His own melody during a 40 day wilderness period. Satan lured him with a satisfying set of values totally opposed to His true source of life. What kind of Messiah would He be? Seductions of power and prestige were laid before Him. Instant gratification. He could be king!

Yet Jesus lived to only one song, that of His father. Our worship is to join that song.

HEALTH SMART

◆ You will likely feel more tired than normal at the end of the day. Get plenty of rest.

VOICES OF WISDOM

❖ "Fasting is better than prayer."

— **St. Clement (ca. 215 A.D.)**

REFLECTIONS

_____

_____

_____

_____

_____

_____

_____

_____

_____

_____

_____

_____

_____

_____

_____

_____

_____

_____

_____

DAY 19

Since I am afflicted and needy, let the Lord be mindful of me.
Thou art my help and my deliverer. (Psa. 40:17)

WITH PLAINNESS AND urgency, *The Message* captures the prayer of verse 17 in this way: "And me? I'm a mess. I'm nothing and have nothing: make something of me."

Can you identify with that cry?

Make something of me.

We want to do great things, and then we fail at little things. We want to be bold and then we are timid. We want to please God. We want to do our fast *well.* As has been previously discussed, however, fasting is not about us impressing God. We fast either because 1) we are in need of God; or 2) we have grown dull to our need of God, and wish to come to our senses. In either case, hunger is the path to recognition, the doorway to clarity, the key to passion.

If you know you need God, get hungry. If you're sick of self-sufficient toil and striving, get hungry. Psalm 40:17 is for those in the first group. In this group, we know we're a mess. We feel overlooked, left behind, misunderstood. We can't break our jealous streak, our angry outbursts, our lust for just one more glimpse of porn. Just one, that's all! We try to deny homosexual impulses. We have a past that embarrasses us. We curse under our breath at traffic and then wonder if we will ever get ahead on our bills. We're drowning in grief, yet no one knows how to comfort us. Maybe no one even cares. Maybe we feel nameless, useless and completely unworthy. We dread looking in the mirror because failure stares right back at us.

What could *we* possibly offer a holy God? The very thought mocks us. And yet . . . hope against hope we cry out: *Please, God! Make something of me!*

It almost seems silly. But we don't give up.

Make something of me.

Friend, this is a good thing, and greatly pleasing to the Lord. Though we may feel inadequate, it is not He who shames us. He delights in the weakest among us with the same fervency and joy He showers upon the greatest, the most anointed, the most steady, the most virtuous.

A man stood on the street corner, thumped his chest and boasted to himself about how good and godly he was. Truth be told, he probably was a very "together" kind of person. The record shows he was a tithing, fasting, God-fearing, law-keeping pillar of the community. By contrast, another man wept in his closet over the depth of his sins. Truth be told, he probably was a mess; a scoundrel and a cheat (Luke 18:10-14).

But wait.

Which one did God justify?

Whose prayers did God receive?

Fall hard on mercy. Never give up the cry of a broken heart. Never doubt the fierce love of a kind God. Are you afflicted and in need?

He *will* help. He *will* deliver.

Note: I want to dole out big, heaping helpings of grace for anyone who tries and fails to complete their forty days. A friend of mine did a 21 day fast. On Day 20, he happened to pass through the kitchen where his wife had just baked a fresh loaf of bread. A thought popped into his head: *Communion! I'll just take communion. That's a good thing to do.* By the time it was over, the whole loaf was gone. Yes, it happens to just about everyone who chooses to fast. You set your heart toward the Lord, you turn your gaze upon Him and that alone makes His heart beat faster (Song 4:9). Don't get discouraged or beat yourself up. It's a journey *and* a destination. Just try again, maybe attempting a ten day fast next time. Trust His love for you and keep going. We see the failure, God sees the heart.

FAITH TIP

✓ You will have weak days and strong days. If you begin to despair, ask for grace, dig into the Word. Hold your ground until the hunger wave or panicked feeling passes. If you're bored, find a creative outlet in which you can expend energy.

VOICES OF WISDOM

❖ There is nothing which so certifies the genuineness of a man's faith as his patience and his patient endurance, his keeping on steadily in spite of everything."

— **Martyn Lloyd-Jones (1899-1981)**

REFLECTIONS

_____

_____

_____

_____

_____

_____

_____

_____

_____

_____

DAY 20

Do not delay, O my God (Psa. 40:17)

TIME IS LINEAR, but relative. Time is felt, but invisible. The passage of time is both a puzzle beyond reckoning and a plain fact of life we barely notice. When we do perceive it, it is in the cycles of light and darkness, day and night; we feel its weight when present moments become past memories. We experience it as a series of events, or as wrinkles and scars on our skin. We symbolize it with clocks, calendars, hourglasses.

We don't often think of food as a timekeeper . . . until you fast. You never realize how much variety meal time and meal flavors add to your day until they are utterly absent from your routine. Days *lengthen* without food breaks. More than anything else, it is food that divides our hours into morning, noon and evening. Like little goal posts, meals reward us for the passage of time.

Thus, on a physical and mental level, fasting can become monotonous in the extreme. Our spirit must be trained to flourish, to seize the opportunities it is given while the flesh is being tamed. Our mind must practice finding other outlets for creativity and energy.

To experience the inertial drag of fasting is to volunteer for the tutelage of patience. Twenty days ago this journey started with a declaration that we would wait patiently for the Lord. Each word was key. Wait. Patiently. For Him. It was not yet time to ask for acceleration. A major goal of the inward journey of fasting is entirely circumvented if we grow impatient with the process.

You see, when we cut loose from the temporary pleasure of food, we are liberated to more freely hunger for *eternal* things. To eternalize our hunger is to more accurately perceive our condition. Generally, when humans hunger in spirit, we translate the urge as requiring immediate satisfaction. We interpret these quiet impulses, these longings, as something to be appeased, be they hungerings for significance, beauty, fascination, love, approval, respect, understanding. Though these deeply human realities are comparable in worth to diamonds, yet we treat them as lumps of coal made for a common fire. By this I mean we search for (and find) gratification all too easily. No mistake could be easier to make. The world is all too happy to accommodate our eternal needs with superficial pleasures.

During an extended fast, we find our most casual, well-worn gratification paths blocked. We pine for the simple act of chewing like it is a long lost friend. This hunger is a gift to our deepest selves, for it gently guides us into the realm of eternal things.

Thankfully, in the fast, we have no such recourse. We find that our most casual, well-worn paths to gratification have all been blocked. Utterly thwarted. No food for the belly, no taste on the tongue. We pine for the simple act of chewing like it is a long lost friend. This hunger, though pain to our flesh, is a gift to our deepest selves, for it gently guides us into the realm of eternal things. There we discover our soul, panting for God. There we find

God, waiting for us more than we for Him. It is an experience you cannot recreate at the buffet line.

Fasting distills. Feasting dilutes. It is a paradox, but true.

So in the midst of this, you realize you have come to the halfway mark of your forty days and forty nights. Today is day 20. This is a fair turning point. You cannot quite let yourself grow restless yet, or panicky feelings might overtake you and perhaps ruin everything.

Even so, it is a good time to begin feeling the importance of the things the Lord has revealed thus far. You carry promises in the Word, in your bosom. You carry burdens. You seek release. You have tasted defeat in the past, you have mourned and grieved and waited for the tides to turn. They have not turned. At least not yet. Breakthrough awaits.

"God, don't put it off!" David cries in *The Message*. "Get going!"

It's good to let a bit of urgency rise in your spirit. The eternal, though unmoved by the passage of time, must consume it before all is said and done. The Kingdom stands at the threshold, waiting to penetrate our lives with fresh conviction, fresh hope, fresh anointing.

"Thy Kingdom come, Thy will be done . . . "

Where? On *earth*. Here, now. In this time. As it is in the eternal perfection of heaven.

No more delays, God. Come!

HEALTH SMART

✦ As your body detoxifies, an emotional cleansing may begin to occur in parallel. It is not uncommon to experience a heightened emotional response, as negative emotional habits are accentuated. In addition, feelings attached to past woundings might strangely resurface with a freshness and vitality that may surprise you. While frustrating, this should be viewed as an opportunity to surrender poisoned emotions and memories to the Lord for healing and restoration.

VOICES OF WISDOM

❖ "Afflictions are light when compared with what we really deserve. They are light when compared with the sufferings of the Lord Jesus. But perhaps their real lightness is best seen by comparing them with the weight of glory which is awaiting us.

— **A.W. Pink (1886-1952)**

REFLECTIONS

_____

_____

_____

_____

_____

_____

_____

_____

_____

_____

_____

REBIRTH

"Repent therefore and return, that your sins may be wiped away, in order that times of refreshing may come from the presence of the Lord"

— **Peter the Apostle**

DAY 21

Speak kindly to Jerusalem; and call out to her, that her warfare has ended, that her iniquity has been removed, that she has received of the Lord's hand double for all her sins. (Isa. 40:2)

I HOPE IT IS evident by now that this is *not* a book about fasting. It is a book of love for Jesus.

Likewise, it is not so much about repentance as renewal. Rebirth. Each day of your forty days and forty nights holds the potential for twenty-four more hours of lovesickness as you learn to long for a beautiful God-man who breaks into human history with stunning kindness and power. He breaks into your history, mine, the earth's, because nothing can tame the wild love of this holy God.

Amazingly, He does so even when our choices grossly conflict with His goodness. Do you know that? Do you know His actions of love? They are evident to tender, grateful hearts, yet how easily we grow dull, entitled and selfish! Do we *see* His patient, ransoming work? Or like cataracts and glaucoma, has our vision grown cloudy and dull? Do we have ears to hear or are we deaf?

Friends, we are far too casual in assessing our current state of affairs. It is a dangerous Laodicean error to believe material blessing equals spiritual depth, or that the favor God generously bestows always demonstrates we are in right alignment with His Word. In reality, we all tolerate minor rebellions against the gracious rulership of Jesus. We are *all* guilty, right down to how we spend our money and use our time. Each of us seem perpetually stuck in teenage-hood—full of willfulness, bent on pursuing *our* ideas, *our* plans. We must grow up.

Take a moment to be honest with yourself. As His disciple, do you actively or passively respond to His word? Do you listen to His voice with a heart of ready, quick obedience, or only when it suits your inclinations without causing any real discomfort? Beloved, it is not right that we behave so flippantly when we have been bought at such a great cost. It is more than *un*right, it is unjust. The world is broken and we broke it. Apart from grace, is it any wonder that we should reap the full consequence of our rebellion right down to the smallest details of our lives?

From the vantage point of the courts of Heaven, what is the verdict on the Church in America? Is it possible that we have earned the opposition of almighty God? Let us not be too proud or hasty to dismiss the possibility. The children of Israel experienced His discipline in terrifying ways.

God said, "For forty years—one year for each of the forty days you explored the land—you will suffer for your sins and *know what it is like to have me against you*" (Num. 14:34).

Could a more dreadful pronouncement be uttered? Yet we are in a different covenant. He deals with us in love as His children, not His enemies. Yet His desire to guide, correct and bless remains. What would be unloving is for God to leave us on our unwitting, lackadaisical path to destruction. The end of the age is upon us, and we are not prepared! The antichrist spirit looms large in the world. Are you ready? Are your robes white, your lamps trimmed, your vessel full of oil? If not, how will you get there? What must change?

Those who do not walk in friendship with God *will* feel His heavy hand as a manifestation of His jealous, redemptive love. It is kindness and severity, all at once. For decades now, we have felt it in our nation. Our families, finances, perhaps even our physical bodies have known what it is like for the Lord to remove His hand of protection. For three years prior to this fast, I felt like God and I were opponents in a boxing ring, rather than companions on the battlefield. I was sluggish of spirit, overweight physically, disconnected emotionally, and generally dull to the ways of God. Every day repeated my cycle of discouragement.

Then, with great faithfulness, longsuffering and patience towards me—even *today,* with fresh new mercy—His voice rises in the midst of my fast. I hear the kind voice of God calling out to me, preemptively declaring that our contest is actually over and He wins (He had all along).

Because He wins, I win.

It is too good to be true. But it is true. Because of a wooden stake buried in the ground 2000 years ago like a dagger planted in the dark heart of sin—a dagger shaped like a cross—a double penalty has been paid, and I inherit righteousness.

"There my burdened soul found liberty, at Calvary."

I begin to bless even my bruises, for they have helped bring me to my senses

Though I have felt his heavy hand, it has never been His anger against me. Rather, it is the equivalent of me running into a concrete wall over and over and again, then finally noticing that I'm sore and bruised and deciding I don't really want to do that anymore. He has not changed. But I have. And when I awaken to His unmovable, sovereign goodness, when I agree with *that,* I begin to bless the bruises, for they have in fact helped bring me to my senses.

Friends, in such a time as this, we cannot afford to go our own way. We must follow His.

FAITH TIP

VOICES OF WISDOM

✓ Spend time today in devotional prayer. Meditate on what it means for your warfare to be ended. Proactively thank Him that your iniquity has been removed.

❖ "Fasting with a pure heart and motives, I have discovered, brings personal revival and adds power to our prayers. Personal revival occurs because fasting is an act of humility. Fasting gives opportunity for deeper humility as we recognize our sins, repent, receive God's forgiveness, and experience His cleansing of our soul and spirit."

— Bill Bright (1921-2003)

REFLECTIONS

_____

_____

_____

_____

_____

_____

_____

_____

_____

_____

_____

_____

_____

DAY 22

A voice is calling (Isa. 40:3)

IN THE BEGINNING, God spoke. At the sound of His voice, which Scripture reveals to be the reality of Christ manifest into creation itself (John 1:3, Col. 1:16-17), worlds were flung into the void. The universe was born, brimming with stars, galaxies and wonder. Green things, animals, humankind. Life was born.

On a dark night splattered with those same stars, the voice spoke again, this time to a man called Abram. He was told to count the stars if he could. That would be the number of his descendants. Children born. Nations created. More life.

In a mountain bush wreathed with unburning fire, the voice spoke again. This time it was about freedom from bondage, a new *quality* of life. Over and over in Scripture, the voice spoke, until finally, on a dusty Judaean landscape, the voice appeared once more. Again, life gushed forth. Divine life followed this Man. Life came from this voice. It still does.

> "God, after He spoke long ago to the fathers in the prophets in many portions and in many ways, in these last days has spoken to us in His Son, whom He appointed heir of all things, through whom also He made the world" (Heb. 1:1-2).

This is the voice we follow, the very word of God. Physically, He is now absent from the earth. But there is good news, He is coming again! Who will bear witness to Him, to His coming? Who knows the voice well enough to speak it on His behalf? The bride uniquely hears the voice of her Beloved. The son uniquely hears the voice of His Father. These identities, sons and corporate bride, help to shape our voice. When we take our place, when we believe He means for us to *be* that kind of people, we will become the carrier and proclaimer of His voice on the earth.

John the Baptist was such a man. He called himself the "friend of the Bridegroom." Jesus said he was the greatest man born of a woman up to that point in history. He called John a burning, shining lamp (John 5:35). John was relentlessly focused on preparing the people for the coming of the Lamb of God. He was the voice prophesied in Malachi 3:1, "'Behold, I am going to send My messenger, and he will clear the way before Me. And the Lord, whom you seek, will suddenly come to His temple; and the messenger of the covenant, in whom you delight, behold, He is coming,' says the Lord of hosts." When someone important is coming, you clean house. John cleaned house.

Jesus said that John was like Elijah (Mat. 11:14). Elijah had an equally fierce spirit. He was jealous for Yahweh's claims upon the earth and labored to purge unfaithfulness from the land. Elijah challenged Jezebel and a host of demonic powers, called down fire, worked miracles, and stood against the tide of darkness in his generation. Jesus said, "My friend, John, he's like that . . . only even more so than Elijah." He was *more* than a prophet (Luke 7:26). John lived a fasted lifestyle. "For John the Baptist has come eating no bread and drinking no wine; and you say, 'He has a demon!' (Luke 7:33). John didn't care; he served the pleasure of God, not men. Bear in mind, it was the *religious leaders* that did this. What will you do when they slander you? John just kept on preaching, baptizing, eating locust. Social etiquette was not his concern. The message was central.

Jesus loved this guy. He talked more favorably about John than any other man in the Bible. Do you know why? It is because

He found a voice completely loyal to His own. He had found a friend, a man of passion, recklessness, intensity and focus; a suitable container for the message of God. Get this: John did not just faithfully speak words, he embodied a message.

That same voice is still calling. Do you hear it? Are you ready to *become* His voice on the earth? Now is the time.

VOICES OF WISDOM

✤ "The goal of fasting is inner unity. This means hearing, but not with the ear; hearing, but not with the understanding; it is hearing with the spirit, with your whole being. The hearing that is only in the ears is one thing. The hearing of the understanding is another, but the hearing of the spirit is not limited to any one faculty, to the ear, or to the mind. Hence, it demands the emptiness of the faculties, and when the faculties are empty, then your whole being listens. There is then a direct grasp of what is right before you that can never be heard with the ear or understood with the mind. Fasting of the heart empties the faculties, frees you from limitations and from preoccupations."

— **Thomas Merton (1915-1968)**

REFLECTIONS

_____

_____

_____

_____

_____

_____

_____

_____

_____

DAY 23

Clear the way for the Lord in the wilderness (Isa. 40:3)

WHAT DOES IT MEAN to clear the way for the Lord? It was John's mission. It must be ours. But what is it? John came as a forerunner; one who goes ahead to prepare for One coming behind. In our own lives, no less across the whole earth, Jesus is committed to clearing a path, removing everything that hinders love. He clears *our* way by the power of the Holy Spirit, who guides us into all truth (John 16:13) and convicts of sin, righteousness and judgment (John 16:8). This is done that we might in turn help to clear a way for the Lord in the midst of the wilderness of this world.

The Jewish tradition leading up to Yom Kippur yields beautiful insight into this aspect of your forty days. Yom Kippur, the Day of Atonement, is the highest holy day on the Jewish calendar. This is hands down the most terrifying day for a Jew, more so even than Passover. An entire month is given to personal preparation plus the Ten Days of Awe (aka 'Rosh HaShanah') immediately prior.

So, 30 + 10 = 40. Over and over, we see that forty is about preparation, testing, transformation.

Okay, enough history. Consider it in these terms. If you knew you were to appear before a judge in a court of law, would you prepare your case or just take your chances? That's what the Day of Atonement is, a day when the scales are weighed and judgment hangs in the balance. Unless God Himself extends mercy, we're done for. So too, the Jews believe they are given the entire month of

Elul to prepare themselves for the coming judgment through self reflection, prayer and repentance. This is not random. Moses spent 40 days fasting and pleading on Mt. Sinai during the month of Elul for Israel's forgiveness after the failure of the golden calf. On the first day of that month, Moses climbed Sinai again and remained there 40 days, interceding. God forgave. Another set of tablets was created. Moses then returned to the people. *That* day, the day of his return, became the Day of Atonement.

Now here's the beautiful part. Jewish tradition teaches that God is somehow more accessible during this 40-day period. A group of rabbis known as the Mystical Sages referred to this period as when "The King is in the Field." The notion is that a king is not easily accessible when enthroned in his palace. A person of unusual standing might be given audience, but not a commoner. However, when the king is out in public, anyone may approach him. He comes out to inspect the borders, the local produce, maybe check on his army . . . *and* to express concern for the well-being of his subjects. When this happens, the King may be approached by the average farmer. Such behavior is expected, actually. The farmer seizes his opportunity to pay respects and express his needs and thoughts to the King. Thus, during these forty days (say the sages), we have the chance to draw unusually close to God. He is most receptive to our prayers. He comes to the mountain, He touches earth. He is near.

Of course, we know our access to the throne of Christ is based upon grace, not timing. Our Day of Atonement is settled in the heavens. We do not have to wait until the Days of Awe. We come boldly as often as needed. Our debt price is paid, the veil is torn, the Holy of Holies has been opened. But there is wisdom here.

"Seek the Lord while He may be found; call upon Him while He is near" (Isa. 55:6).

For 2000 years, our King has been in His field. For 2000 years, you've had free access. Will you seize your moment?

Part of clearing the path of God within is to soberly recognize a coming day of judgement. Jesus said, "We must work the works of Him who sent Me, as long as it is day; night is coming, when no man can work" (John 9:4). We must soberly respond to our moment of grace. We must recognize that for 2000 years, our King has been in His field. How will you seize your moment? You are here, on Day 23, with free access. What should you do?

> *"And this do, knowing the time, that it is already the hour for you to awaken from sleep; for now salvation is nearer to us than when we believed. The night is almost gone, and the day is at hand. Let us therefore lay aside the deeds of darkness and put on the armor of light. Let us behave properly as in the day, not in carousing and drunkenness, not in sexual promiscuity and sensuality, not in strife and jealousy. But put on the Lord Jesus Christ, and make no provision for the flesh in regard to its lusts"* (Rom. 13:11-14).

In other words, clear the way for the Lord.

FAITH TIP

✓ Use your forty days as an extended house cleaning. Remove clutter and distractions from your daily routine. Ask the Lord, what stands in the way of loving You more?

VOICES OF WISDOM

❖ "Is not the neglect of this plain duty—I mean, fasting, ranked by our Lord with almsgiving and prayer—one general occasion of deadness among Christians? Can any one willingly neglect it, and be guiltless?"

— John Wesley (1703-1791)

REFLECTIONS

_____

_____

_____

_____

_____

_____

_____

_____

_____

_____

_____

_____

_____

_____

_____

_____

DAY 24

Make smooth in the desert a highway for our God. (Isa. 40:3)

WE WILL SPEND the next few days and verses exploring various facets of how we respond to the Lord's voice; how we own the message of preparation that we might ourselves declare it. Basically, this means we obey the call to clear a path for the Lord *within ourselves first.*

First we must answer the question, what is this highway? Isaiah previously introduced it a few chapters earlier. "A highway will be there, a roadway, and it will be called the Highway of Holiness. The unclean will not travel on it, but it will be for him who walks that way, and fools will not wander on it . . . and the ransomed of the Lord will return, and come with joyful shouting to Zion (Isa. 35:8,10). The highway is the path of the Lord, the gateway to His presence. It is distinguished by holiness. Proverbs 15:17 agrees: "The highway of the upright is to depart from evil."

But there is a problem. The highway of holiness isn't finished. It's rough. It needs to be smoothed. If you've ever seen new highway construction, you understand why. Roads don't naturally occur. Rocks and rivers, trees and boulders—all kinds of obstacles—require systematic removal. Country roads don't require as much effort, but neither do they enjoy the same volume of traffic and size of freight. Semis don't travel down dirt roads, they travel wide four-lane interstates. Likewise, the scope of our cooperation with God in preparing our own highway significantly limits or expands the life of God we operate in, the ministry we are entrusted with, and the impact of our lives for the Kingdom. An airport runway makes the point even more dramatically. Do you want a little 2-prop Cesna of God, or do you want to land C-35 transports and 747s? I want to be able to radio in as big of an aircraft as possible. That takes length, breadth, surface preparation, extra foundation depth, stronger materials and time. It doesn't happen overnight.

Next we must ask, *where* is this highway? In Psalm 84, David spoke of another highway, but it is really the same one. *"How blessed is the man whose strength is in Thee; in whose heart are the highways to Zion!"* (Psa. 83:5). In both references, the path leads to Zion.

Where is the highway to Zion?
Ultimately, we are meant to understand that the highway to Zion—that place of rulership, sacrifice and the law of God—lies within by the work of the Holy Spirit.

Now we must ask, what is Zion? Some scholars argue for Zion as the colloquial name given to King David's throne in Jerusalem. Others say Zion is specifically Mt. Moriah, one of Jerusalem's four mountains, where Abraham committed the *Aqedah*, the binding of Isaac, and where Solomon's Temple was later built. Generically, it came to refer to the whole of Jerusalem, which literally means City of Peace. It is the geographic epicenter of God's dealings with earth.

"For the law will go forth from Zion, and the word of the Lord from Jerusalem" (Isa. 2:3).

This helps us understand David's revelation, that the highway to Zion—that place of rulership, sacrifice and the law of God—lies right within our heart. By the work of the Holy Spirit within, we have a fountainhead of life. Here, Jesus said, "from (your) innermost being shall flow rivers of living water" (John 7:38). The heart is a highway. The heart is a wellspring of life. The Lordship of Jesus is ever-present, but we get clogged. The water can't flow. We have to clear the path.

As we shall see, this highway is meant to produce an increasing bounty of fresh revelation of the many splendors of Jesus. But we're only landing Cesnas, because our preparation in holiness is incomplete. We have yet to create a runway big enough for a true, end-time revelation of Jesus.

> *"And I, brethren, could not speak to you as to spiritual men, but as to men of flesh, as to babes in Christ. I gave you milk to drink, not solid food; for you were not yet able to receive it. Indeed, even now you are not yet able, for you are still fleshly"* (1 Cor. 3:1-3).

Implicit in this rebuke is a promise of greater revelation to come when fleshly impulses are sufficiently dealt with. You understand this, you hunger for it, or you wouldn't have made it to Day 24. Now go deeper. Ask God what practical sacrifices He would ask of you, even beyond food. If you have the grace for it, make a Mt. Moriah moment for the remainder of your fast. Lay down Isaac, who was not evil, but good! It was a test of faith.

Embrace the challenge to clear your highway. Above all, keep going!

FAITH TIP

✓ In a long fast, it is tempting to distract yourself in an effort to minimize the boredom you will experience. Resist this urge. We consume so much garbage in what we see with our eyes and hear with our ears. Get rid of it! Let yourself hunger for Jesus and Jesus alone.

VOICES OF WISDOM

✤ "Fasting, if we conceive of it truly, must not . . . be confined to the question of food and drink; fasting should really be made to include abstinence from anything which is legitimate in and of itself for the sake of some special spiritual purpose. There are many bodily functions which are right and normal and perfectly legitimate, but which for special peculiar reasons in certain circumstances should be controlled. That is fasting."

— **Martyn Lloyd-Jones (1899-1981)**

REFLECTIONS

DAY 25

Let every valley be lifted up (Isa. 40:4)

THE IMAGERY OF the heart being a highway into Zion, the seat of the King, is powerful. But equally meaningful is the next verse, wherein those whose hearts have become this highway and have touched the grace of God are empowered to turn a valley of weeping into a source of life.

> *"Passing through the valley of Baca, they make it a spring. The early rain also covers it with blessings. They go from strength to strength, every one of them appears before God in Zion"* (Psa. 84:6)

'Baca' means weeping, as some translations render it. In the valley of weeping, this strange conversion happens, from sorrow to joy. It says the rain comes with blessings. Strength increases. This is beautiful language, but what does it all mean? What's really going on here?

Perhaps we should first ask, what is a valley? In basic geographical terms, a valley is that place where the earth is torn between two higher elevations—typically hills or mountains. Mountains can represent kingdoms; also pride. Most commonly, they depict lofty experiences, high vision, revelation, clarity. We speak of great moments as "mountaintop experiences"—pinnacle moments of triumph and blessing. On a mountaintop, you see farther. You are raised up.

Conversely, valleys are the low places where we are tempted to despair. Famously in Psalm 23, it was "in the valley of the shadow of death," that David said he found the comfort and courage not to fear. But it was still a valley. Megiddo, the famous location of the apocalyptic last battle from whence Armageddon derives its name, is part of the wider Valley of Jezreel. It has been and will be a place of conflict and sorrow. It represents a seemingly impossible situation.

The tears of those who weep carry the very essence of the next surge of mercy from a loving God. Life happens—sometimes good, sometimes bad—but always, mercy flows from high to low. This is why valleys are typically lush, fertile gardens of life.

Now get this: in the economy of God, it is the valley *to which all the mountain waters flow!* You see, a mountaintop may contain vision and victory, but it cannot contain water, and water is life. Gravity demands that the high place *must* supply the valley beneath it. Those who weep carry within their very tears the essence of the next surge of mercy from a loving God. Life happens —sometimes good, sometimes bad, but mercy always flows down from the high places. This is why valleys are typically lush, fertile gardens of life. They naturally attract and retain what a mountain is incapable of holding. We don't think of weeping and mourning as joyful events for a simple reason, they aren't. Yet they tenderize and fertilize our souls with the necessary ingredients for the next wave of joy. Rains, blessings and new strength are discovered there. Yes, it's painful. It can be *so* painful! So don't hold back. Weep! Cry out! Pour out your heart. Just remember, Psa. 84 says you're just "passing through" this place. Go read it again. You *will* get to the other side.

"The nights of crying your eyes out give way to days of laughter. (God) did it: changed wild lament into whirling dance; You ripped off my black mourning band and decked me with wildflowers" (Psa. 30:5,11; MSG)

The merciful heart of God is lovingly focused on those struggling in the valley. Where our world is torn, we weep. Thankfully, fundamental to preparing His highway inside us is the process of actually raising our valleys. The action of grace brings healing. Perpetually wounded forerunners have broken voices and will declare faulty messages. So before God deals with the "high places," He graciously replaces the pain of our low places. The highway to Zion cannot be full of potholes. Where we have been crushed, God will bring healing. If you feel lost in a place of despair, know this: God is in motion to bring comfort to past wounds and present disappointments. While a forerunner like John the Baptist can only be prepared in a furnace of suffering, it must not turn into bitterness, cynicism or unending despair. Jesus was bruised and whipped, beaten and pierced, rejected and mocked, slandered and betrayed, forgotten and reviled . . . and then He forgave.

"The Lord is near to the brokenhearted, and saves those who are crushed in spirit" (Psa. 34:18) . . . .if your heart is broken, you'll find God right there; if you're kicked in the gut, he'll help you catch your breath" (MSG).

FAITH TIP

✓ Even "good things" can distract us, ultimately diluting the intensity of our love for God. They aren't morally wrong, but is it worth it for the good to hinder the better as we long for His best? Contemporary disciples of Jesus are thoroughly distracted. What distracts your devotion? Choose to be still before the Lord with no agenda and no props. Take off the iPod earbuds. Log of the computer. Wait on Him. See what happens.

VOICES OF WISDOM

❖ "Detachment from the confusion all around us is in order to have a richer attachment to God. Christian meditation leads us to the inner wholeness necessary to give ourselves to God freely."

— **Richard Foster**

❖ "Fasting is the single greatest natural healing therapy. It is nature's ancient, universal 'remedy' for many problems."

— **Elson Haas, M.D.**

REFLECTIONS

_____

_____

_____

_____

_____

_____

_____

_____

_____

_____

_____

_____

_____

DAY 26

And every mountain and hill be made low (Isa. 40:4)

IF A WOUNDED forerunner delivers a faulty message, a proud forerunner risks proclaiming something worse: himself. Oh beloved, we would be hard pressed to find anything more opposed by God than pride. Let me put it bluntly. *Pride is the anointing of Satan.* It is not trivial, like poor manners. It is an abomination to Him (Prov. 16:5). If grace is the favor of God, pride is the favor of damnation. It is the original sin of the fallen cherub, causing fallen man to stink with the odors of hell. It taints *everything*. We are far too tolerant of its corrupting power. By pride we self-justify, oppress, boast, rebel, mock, disobey, lust, neglect, use, scheme, grow jealous, angry and plot our advancement. It is the inspiration behind every other vice; a noxious weed with branching, fine-haired roots running so deep through every facet of human personality that our only recourse is to vigilantly submit our entire person to the mercy of God and the prevailing reality of Christ, every day. All pride and personal ambition must be humbled if we are to become the voice of the Lord to our generation. Jesus is the star of the show, not us. *He* is our message. For inspiration on how this is achieved, John the Baptist once again shines:

> *"John answered, 'A man can receive nothing, unless it has been given him from heaven. You yourselves bear me witness, that I said, 'I am not the Christ,' but, 'I have been sent before Him.' He who has the bride is the bridegroom; but the friend of the bridegroom, who stands and hears*

him, rejoices greatly because of the bridegroom's voice. And so this joy of mine has been made full. He must increase, but I must decrease.'" (John 3:27-30)

Bear in mind, when John said this he was having his own mountaintop experience. He was at the peak of popularity, baptizing thousands in the Jordan. His "ministry" was well-known and well-respected. Throngs flocked miles into the desert to hear him preach. Some were even asking if *he* was the Messiah. Pretty heady stuff.

John shook it off. He had a clear mandate: *He must increase. I must decrease.*

In the revelation of Jesus, John found gladness.

It was in the revelation of Jesus that John found gladness. He rejoiced in the promotion of the Lamb more than himself. He didn't just say, "May God be glorified." He added to it, "And let me fade away altogether."

This is what it means to make the mountains low. Our own glory, our own achievement, our own potential must diminish. The high places of our pride must be brought low. A highway is being built inside the soul of every true disciple. However, if you aspire to be a voice, a forerunner to the church and the world as John was, the building code becomes even more strict. John was an extremist. He wasn't looking to win any 'Mr. Congeniality' contests. Public Relations was not his strength. His virtue was that he burned for the Messiah above anything his talents might have gained himself. With reckless disregard for the undercutting of his own influence, he proclaimed, "Behold the Lamb . . . I'm not even worthy to untie his sandals."

Pride, wrecked. Satan's anointing, crushed.

In its place, all around smelly Jordan, the rich fragrance of humility filled the air, which meant the stage was set for Christ to be revealed. Every eye turned from John to Jesus. Just as John intended, they beheld *Him*. Mission accomplished.

Your mission, my mission, is no more, no less than that. Reveal Jesus.

As we become familiar with how God builds His "Presence Highway" within us, we become engineers in the construction of that global superhighway that will soon usher in the fullness of His Kingdom on earth.

We are in training—mountain wrecking, valley raising training. As we become versed in how God builds the highway of His presence within, we become engineers in the construction of that global superhighway that will soon usher in the fullness of the Kingdom of God.

But don't kid yourself. The massive scope of this final highway requires massive personal investment. Forty days is a good beginning, but it is only a beginning. Do you grasp the scale of what we are a part of? The highway of God leads right through the end of the age and terminates at the Second Coming of the King of Kings.

FAITH TIP

✓ As the Lord renews you emotionally and spiritually, it is important to receive the confidence of His actions on your behalf. Every day, go before Him in a posture of submission and need, but do not only confess what you lack, thank Him for what He supplies. Confess the truth of your identity in Christ. As you ask for mercy and grace for true, inward change, also meditate with hope on the fact that He makes all things new. You are safe in Him.

VOICES OF WISDOM

❖ "There is too much sleep, too much meat and drink, too little fasting and self-denial, too much taking part in the world . . . and too little self-examination and prayer."

— **William Bramwell (1856-1929)**

REFLECTIONS

_____

_____

_____

_____

_____

_____

_____

_____

_____

_____

_____

_____

DAY 27

*Let the rough ground become a plain, and the rugged terrain
a broad valley. Then the glory of the Lord will be revealed*
(Isa. 40:4-5)

THERE IT IS! The glory of the Lord *will* be revealed.

But notice, within the context of what has come before, this verse sets qualifications for our participation in that glory. Everything prior is crucial preparation, not optional. It is only after the raising, lowering, smoothing and flattening of the rough ground—after investing time and emotion, responding to the Holy Spirit's conviction, getting old wounds healed, facing sin habits head-on, choosing humility over pride—after that process, *then* the glory of the Lord will be revealed.

This isn't an easy path. Your flesh will hate it because you must constantly bring those old, carnal behaviors to their full death on the cross. Jesus said, *"If anyone wishes to come after Me, let him deny himself, and take up his cross daily"* (Luke 9:23). Highlight that word. Daily, we must grab hold of the resurrection life of Christ, apply it to our lives and reject everything that is anti-life. Why would we wish to return to the slavery from which we have been delivered? We possess a new nature! But to fully inhabit that promise, we must daily put on Christ (Rom. 13:14). This is why fasting is an indispensable training tool. Fasting 1) trains you to a lifestyle of persistent discipline toward your most basic and pervasive appetite, eating; 2) it serves to weaken the overall will of your flesh, thus enabling you to more successfully apply spiritual restraint to other areas; and 3) it tenderizes your heart to the Holy Spirit, on whom you must utterly depend for real, lasting transformation.

> "Therefore consider the members of your earthly body as dead to immorality, impurity, passion, evil desire, and greed, which amounts to idolatry" (Col. 3:5) . . . for if you are living according to the flesh, you must die; but if by the Spirit you are putting to death the deeds of the body, you will live" (Rom. 8:13) . . . therefore do not let sin reign in your mortal body that you should obey its lusts" (Rom. 6:12).

Paul's idea of the human body was to see it as the fulfillment of everything the Old Covenant temple represented. Both the tabernacle and temple were physical reservoirs of God's presence on earth. Amazingly, _you_ are the fulfillment of those types.

Of course, the good news is that as this process unfolds, you are increasingly liberated into experiencing the life of Christ. Jesus said, _"You shall be free indeed"_ (John 8:36). The process requires time, endurance, a certain godly stubbornness and a heart willing to receive both the correction and the kindness of God. But it's worth it. "Wisdom is vindicated by all her children" (John 7:35). The fruit of righteousness yields a harvest of blessing in your life. As the temple of the Lord, your body becomes a fit vessel for greater dimensions of supernatural activity.

Paul's revelation of the human body was that it was the fulfillment of everything the Old Covenant temple represented.

The tabernacle of Moses, the temple of Solomon: both were the physical reservoirs of God's presence on planet earth. The old temple was the type. Amazingly, *you* are the fulfillment, the new temple. "Do you not know that you are a temple of God, and that the Spirit of God dwells in you?" (1 Cor. 3:16).

God's glory filled His temple (2 Chron. 5:14; 7:1-3). It filled Jesus, who also referred to His body as the temple of God (John 2:21). Likewise, you are meant to bear the weight of His glory, to manifest His nature in the earth. We are meant to fulfill the Disciple's Prayer, that His kingdom would come on earth as it is in heaven. But there is a problem. As Israel's history sadly demonstrates, the temple can become defiled. This can occur through outright rebellion and the judgments which follow, or merely habitual neglect. In either event, the house of God must be cleansed, as Nehemiah and Ezra understood, and Haggai and Zechariah prophesied. This was the mission of the exiles: rebuild the temple, clean house. This is the mission of fasting, to clean house.

"Or do you not know that your body is a temple of the Holy Spirit . . . *therefore glorify God in your body*" (1 Cor. 6:19-20). Fasting is kindness to our body compared to the enormous health consequences of gluttony. When we glorify Him in his temple, He responds. He moves with power. He arrives. Even if it is hard, it is good. Paul said, "I consider that the sufferings of this present time are not worthy to be compared with *the glory that is to be revealed to us*" (Rom. 8:18).

If you give yourself fully to this for the rest of your life, as long as it takes, at some point the *then* of Isa. 40:5 happens. Glory is revealed.

FAITH TIP

✓ Don't be shy or timid. Partial or even significant victory in an area of addiction or failure is not yet total victory. Bring even the little things into your conversation with God, those small wandering moments scattered throughout a typical day, when your words, attitudes or actions fail to reflect the character of Christ within.

VOICES OF WISDOM

✣ "There is both a physical and a spiritual fast. In the physical fast, the body abstains from food and drink. In the spiritual fast, the faster abstains from evil intentions, words and deeds. By fasting, it is possible both to be delivered from future evils, and to enjoy the good things to come. We fell into disease through sin; let us receive healing through repentance, which is not fruitful without fasting."

— **St. Basil of Caesarea (329-379)**

REFLECTIONS

_____

_____

_____

_____

_____

_____

_____

_____

_____

_____

_____

_____

DAY 28

*All flesh is grass, and all its loveliness is like the flower
of the field. The grass withers, the flower fades, when the
breath of the Lord blows upon it* (Isa. 40:6-7)

Obviously, THIS IS A statement regarding the timeless sovereignty of God as compared to the plans of man, which come to nought. God is eternal. He endures forever. By contrast, man lives and dies. One could ask, what does it all really matter then? In Isaiah 22, God called the people to repent, but instead there was "eating of meat and drinking of wine: 'Let us eat and drink, for tomorrow we may die'" (v. 13). If all flesh is fading grass, doomed to wither and be gone, does our discipline and restraint really matter? Why forty days? These are important questions.

To answer them we must root ourselves in the sovereignty of God. Let's seek God for a broader, more long-term perspective for the path we've chosen, beginning with the call to life.

To be "born again" is not random phrasing, but a description of reality. The moment this happens in the soul of a person, that person is literally born *again,* meaning born into a different quality and construct of life. You move from being a natural creature to a supernatural creature. You move from temporal to eternal. You are recreated, made alive. You might have thought you were alive before, but afterwards you realize you weren't. Another dimension has beckoned your dead spirit to live in fellowship with God. It is a staggering event and happens thousands of times a day all over the globe. There, it just happened again; somewhere, a new creation was born. Each time, as angels bear witness, they are awestruck and dumbfounded that frail humans can be elevated to the nobility and virtue of the Son of God, trading death rags for eternal life.

This action is complete, as a seed is the complete realization of the beautiful plant it will become. But as with a seed, evidence of completion is a function of time and environment. Fullness can be encouraged or discouraged. Maturation can thrive or falter. What sprouts must build its root system in the soil of temporal conflict and the constant reminders of our fleshly origins. Though we are truly born again as citizens of heaven, our residency is planet earth. Life operates parallel to eternity inside a world-system that does not recognize the lordship of Jesus. This battle is philosophical and spiritual, but we feel it most acutely in our mind and flesh. We are not yet changed into the fullness of resurrection, when our body finally becomes every bit as alive with eternal life as our spirit is now with Christ. "Grass-flesh" no more!

While this is currently the Now/Not Yet reality of His kingdom, at the end of the age the process will accelerate until all is finally subsumed in the perfection of His will. Jesus used a broad, evocative term for this increasing intensity: birth pangs. Paul made birth pangs an issue of sonship when he said *the anxious longing of the creation waits eagerly for the revealing of the sons of God*" (Rom. 8:19). We are meant to come into the full inheritance of our identity as sons. It is part of our full redemption. But here's the interesting part. Jesus was also revealed as a Son. Do you know how? By what evidence did Paul say the firstborn Son was revealed? The answer may surprise you. Not the virgin birth, not the miracles. He said the prophets spoke, "concerning His Son . . . who was *declared the Son of God with power by the resurrection from the dead*" (Rom. 1:3-4; also hinted in Acts: 13:33). Jesus himself made a similar claim. When the Jews asked Him for a sign that He was the Messiah, He pointed them to His coming resurrection (John 2:19).

○────────────────────────────────────○

Life operates parallel to eternity. What you invest in now produces eternal yield, manifested one day in the form of your resurrection. In that day, you too will be revealed as a son of God, a younger brother to the Firstborn.

Here's the point. What you are investing in now, even in the temporal framework of "flesh like grass," has an eternal yield, manifested one day in the form of your resurrection. In that day, you too will be revealed as a son of God, a younger brother to Jesus, Who also denied the pleasures of the world for the greater joy of obedience. You carry His promise within as a seed—the very seed of Christ. As He died and rose again to an entirely new kind of physical life, so it is with us. But we must nurture and care for the seed of His life within. Fasting emulates the Lord we love and serve. Out of lovesick mourning for Him, we deny pleasures that might otherwise satisfy, lest we forget how much we miss Him. By this we live beyond the confines of a beautiful, temporary world. We may still have bodies of grass, but we are no longer temporal creatures. The world cannot claim us.

FAITH TIP

✓ "We have this treasure in earthen vessels, that the surpassing greatness of the power may be of God and not from ourselves" (2 Cor. 4:7).

VOICES OF WISDOM

❖ "The greatest of the virtues is prayer, while their foundation is fasting. The reason that fasting has an effect on the spirits of evil rests in its powerful effect on our own spirit. A body subdued by fasting brings the human spirit freedom, strength, sobriety, purity, and keen discernment."

— **St. Ignaty Brianchaninov (1807-1867)**

REFLECTIONS

_____

_____

_____

_____

_____

_____

_____

_____

_____

_____

_____

_____

_____

_____

_____

_____

DAY 29

*The grass withers, the flower fades, but the word of
our God stands forever.* (Isa. 40:8)

THE WORD IS THE revelatory substance of an eternal God. It
is the unmovable pillar upon which the universe rests, defining for
all ages Who God is and what He does. It is both the codified
expression of the Father's unalterable will and the definition of His
unchanging purpose. It reveals Christ, Who from the very
beginning was the Word of God. It is the primary objective of the
Holy Spirit to conform us to this Word; the sword by which He
equips mortal man for the task of living an eternal kind of life. If all
flesh is grass and the grass withers, the Word is the means by
which we unshackle ourselves from the domination of *now* and
become oriented with eternal purpose. The Word eternalizes our
spirit. We may have to drag our unwilling flesh to this feast of
spiritual life, but drag it we shall, one day at a time.

You are on Day 29 of this journey. It is time to smash idols.

The attraction we feel to false gods stands in direct
opposition to the eternal, liberating influence of the Word. In the
form of Scripture, the Word is a material gift promising life. It is ink
and paper, but it is really a conduit of God's Spirit to ours.

Idols are also material. Idols also promise life, but they lie.
They deceive. By life, they mean pleasure. By pleasure they mean
bondage. By bondage they mean death. Idols keep us trapped in
what is passing away, so that we can never be satisfied and always
want more. This is the nature of addiction.

○————————————————————————○

"Christian idols" mostly find their basis in the natural order of God. As ancient pagans worshipped things which echoed God's glory—sun, moon, stars—we make idols out of things which God designed to bless us, but through which the enemy wishes to bring a curse.

If idols did not provide obvious pleasure they would hold no attraction for us. We would see through them; resistance would be easy. "Christian idols" are mostly things that find their basis in the natural order of God. This may seem more polite, but it is nothing new. Ancient pagans made objects of worship out of things that actually revealed God's glory—sun, moon, stars, wind, fire, stone, wood. Likewise, we make idols out of things which God designed to bless us, but which the enemy wishes to curse. He does this by perverting their operation in our lives.

Sex is blessed of God. In marriage.

Food is good for delight and wellness. In moderation.

Money is a fact of life.

Beauty, strength and recreational pursuits are all aspects of our human design, but all of them have specific fields of operation. Boundaries. Outside those boundaries, idols begin to form.

The only way to deal with an idol is to smash it. You don't coax or bargain with one. You don't appease it. An idol, by definition, controls. It receives time, energy, attention, all of which are expressions of worship. Anything that competes with our devotion in the practical aspects of an average day, week or year is potentially an idol. Again, think practically in terms of affection, longing, time, money. *What do you give yourself to?* It could be as simple and innocuous as an excessive TV habit, internet surfing, an obsession for the latest fishing gear, or shopping trips to Macy's. Of course, food is a big, obvious one. Politics is in there. What about sports, body image, exercise junkies? Nothing is wrong with any of these things *within reason,* but we have not yet entered the darker realms of pornography for men, romance fantasies for women, or the unending striving for wealth, power, beauty or acclaim. While God has created a rich world full of blessings to be enjoyed, the modern Christian is so deeply invested in popular culture we don't know the difference between friendship with God and addiction to the world. We defend our heavy involvement with the ambiguity of being "culturally relevant." Typically, these are nothing more than polite excuses for idols we are unwilling to surrender.

Idol worship was the constant downfall of Israel. In every instance, it came about through tolerating idols or idol-worshipping people in their lands. You cannot tolerate an idol, you must destroy it. If you leave any space for them, they will slowly creep back to power and control.

According to Jewish oral tradition, Abraham smashed the idols of his father before leaving the land of Ur to become the father of our faith. Gideon was called to triumph over the Midianites, but before he was allowed to do this God told him to cut down the idols of his father.

This is our path, our forty days. Remove what kills your life in God. Determine that only His Word shall stand.

FAITH TIP

✓ Smash your idols. Turn off the TV. Cancel that magazine subscription. Skip the movie. Just as toxins are being cleansed from body, soul and spirit, toxic elements need to be cleansed from your environment. These can be obvious or subtle, so ask the Lord for a tender spirit, then honestly assess your home and routine without justifying yourself.

VOICES OF WISDOM

❖ "If our principal treasure be as we profess, in things spiritual and heavenly, and woe unto us if it be not so! on them will our affections, and consequently our desires and thoughts, be principally fixed."

— **John Owen (1616-1683)**

REFLECTIONS

_____

_____

_____

_____

_____

_____

_____

_____

_____

_____

_____

_____

_____

DAY 30

Get yourself up on a high mountain, O Zion,
bearer of good news, Lift up your voice mightily ...
Behold, the Lord God will come with might.
Behold, His reward is with Him. (Isa. 40:9-10)

PERHAPS YOU'VE HEARD the story of the old dog chasing a rabbit. After failing to catch the rabbit, the old dog was teased by several younger dogs. After listening to their jeers, the dog barked, "Foolish pups! While I was only running for a meal, that rabbit was running for his life."

Here's the moral: the reward determines the way you run. A meal is a much smaller reward than life. God is not afraid of this truth. In clear and dramatic terms throughout history, God has faithfully proclaimed His reward.

> "God, the Master, comes in power, ready to go into action. He is going to pay back his enemies and reward those who have loved him" (Isa. 40:10, MSG).

David understood this early on. After bringing food to his brothers who were stationed with the armies of Israel, he heard Goliath taunting the people of God. You know the story so well you may never have noticed David's *first* response. Did he rise up to defend God's honor? Was he indignant that the people of God were being disgraced? Yes to both. But those responses came later. First, "David spoke to the men who were standing by him, saying, 'What will be done for the man who kills this Philistine?'" (1 Sam. 17:26).

David's question, in essence: "What's in it for me?" Interesting, don't you think? Remember, this was the man God chose to replace Saul. David was a man after God's own heart. What lesson should we draw from his attitude? I would contend that David's knowledge of the king's promise to give his daughter to the man who triumphed over Goliath was part and parcel of the courage that sent him plunging headlong into the valley of Elah armed with nothing but five stones and faith.

The Hebrews Hall of Faith could not be plainer: "Without faith it is impossible to please Him, for he who comes to God must believe that He is, *and that He is a rewarder of those who seek Him*" (Heb. 11:6).

Do you know what impossible means? It does not mean you've got half a chance. It means *no* chance. Zero, zip, nada. Unless you approach God with a faith construct that includes wanting the reward He gives, He is not pleased. Another way to phrase this is, "Hope for reward is the evidence of faith, which is part of pleasing God."

Most Christians struggle with this. Seeming to anticipate our hesitation, God made sure to place the verse right in Hebrews 11. The clear implication is that all of those listed as heroes were motivated in their faith by a hope for reward. Like David facing Goliath, they understood something important about how to face the challenges of life. We can't truly come to God (in the passionate manner He longs for) unless we truly believe in His reward with all our hearts. Reward lends itself to focus, passion and perseverance. Without it, we easily grow discouraged and timid.

Paul quotes Moses to prove this point.

> *"It is written in the Law of Moses, 'You shall not muzzle the ox while he is threshing.' God is not concerned about oxen, is He? Or is He speaking altogether for our sake? Yes, for our sake . . . because the plowman ought to plow in hope, and the thresher to thresh in hope of sharing the crops"* (1 Cor. 9:9-10; also 1 Tim. 5:18).

Does fasting mean you will somehow earn God's favor? Of course not! God could not love you more and He will not love you less.

What do you hope for in this fast? You made the decision to seek God *with* fasting. Does this mean you will somehow earn God's favor? Of course not! God could not love you more than He already does and He will not love you less. Likewise, you are accepted because of the work of Christ, period. Our answer to the promises of God is already "Yes!" in Christ (2 Cor. 1:20). None of this alters His intention to reward those who diligently seek Him.

Yes, the ever-present danger of pride must be guarded against (more on that later). We live in tension because holy ambition and carnal aspirations so easily blend. Even so, if we shrink back in fear of pride more than coming to God as He intends (Heb. 11:6), we will find ourselves motivated toward *false* humility, not authentic, Christ-centered humility. When that happens, we squelch the legitimate stirrings of the Holy Spirit urging man to spiritual achievement. Fasting beckons us to deny the world and discover joy, not to become proud of the triumph of foodlessness.

Let pride be cursed. Let God be praised. He is coming again . . . and His reward is with Him.

FAITH TIP

✓ The safe path of holy ambition is the one ordained by Jesus: "Whoever wishes to be great among you shall be your servant" (Mark 10:43). This was guidance more than rebuke. Do you wish to be great in God? Follow in the Master's footsteps, who "did not regard equality with God a thing to be grasped, but (took) the form of a bond-servant" (Phil 2:3-4).

VOICES OF WISDOM

❖ "Fasting is an effective and safe method of detoxifying the body. . .a technique that wise men have used for centuries to heal the sick. Fast regularly and help the body heal itself and stay well. Give all of your organs a rest. Fasting can help reverse the aging process, and if we use it correctly, we will live longer, happier lives."

— **James Balch, M.D.**

REFLECTIONS

_____

_____

_____

_____

_____

_____

_____

_____

_____

_____

_____

_____

_____

_____

_____

DAY 31

Behold, the nations are like a drop from a bucket,
and are regarded as a speck of dust on the scales . . .
they are regarded by Him as less than nothing and meaningless
(Isa. 40:15, 17)

LET ME PAUSE FOR a moment of confession. You are probably feeling some of the same things I am at this point in our fast, so it may help you to know you are not alone. Today (really, for the last two weeks, but especially today), I am *sick* of water. I'm sick of the taste of my small ration of juice and of the weird, filmy taste in my mouth as my body continues to detoxify. I'm weary of waiting, smelling, thinking, wanting . . . but never tasting. At the same time, I'm deeply troubled by the weakness of my flesh. It pains me to realize I can't think about God for a measly five minutes straight without slobbering at the thought of day 41, when I finally eat again.

Rest assured, these are normal thoughts. We're human. And that's precisely part of the point. We're *human*. God alone is God. He knows our frailty. It would be easy for the baser tendencies of our roller-coaster emotions to reverse the flow of our God-desires and become a little vacuum inside us, sucking all our thoughts back into the Little Bitty World of Me.

How do we re-center once we reach the point where our minds constantly wander, and we begin to doubt our own sincerity? We need help and guidance. Better yet, we need an anchor. We are so easily moved here, there and yon by how we feel.

We analyze how well we think we're chasing God, and if it's good we feel good, and if it's bad we feel bad. Without realizing it, we slip into incessant navel-gazing. Isaiah comes to our rescue in verses 15 and 17. Basically what he says is, "Hey, get over yourself." It stings a little, but it needs to. According to Isaiah, if you take all our accumulated itty-bitty people thoughts all around the globe, multiply it times several billion a day and again times 6000 thousand years... what to you have?

For God, a drop in the bucket. The nations are meaningless specks of dust.

Oh, the merciful deliverance from the tyranny of ME!

Oh, the merciful gift of deliverance from the tyranny of Me.

"For He says to Moses, 'I will have mercy on whom I have mercy, and I will have compassion on whom I have compassion.' So then it does not depend on the man who wills or the man who runs, but on God who has mercy...

"Who are you, O man, who answers back to God? The thing molded will not say to the molder, 'Why did you make me like this,' will it? Or does not the potter have a right over the clay, to make from the same lump one vessel for honorable use, and another for common use?

"What if God, although willing to demonstrate His wrath and to make His power known, endured with much patience vessels of wrath prepared for destruction? And He did so in order that He might make known the riches of His glory upon vessels of mercy, which He prepared beforehand for glory" (Rom. 9:15-16, 20-23).

At this point in our forty days, perhaps the most useful, faith-enriching, God-centering act would be to surrender more deeply to His sovereignty. It is good that you fast. Don't get lost in the mechanics, the superficial, the speculations. He is in control and we aren't. Our lives are in His hands. On the grand scale of human history, entire nations come and go, while God alone remains. Mighty Babylon, Assyria, Greece, Rome . . . all came to ruins. America perhaps should tremble at this, but the disciple of Jesus should have peace and confidence, for their life story has been transferred to an eternal Kingdom, "a city with foundations whose builder and maker is God" (Heb. 11:10).

God is complete. He is undisturbed in His glory. His dominion is not enhanced by your fasting. *You* may be enhanced, but He never changes. If you nervously start to reach the end of your forty days and think, "Have I done this right? It's almost over, is it working? Is there anything I'm missing? I want to eat so badly I feel like a failure. What else should I do?"

No, no. Don't do. *Be*. His dominion is not diminished by your fasting fluctuations. Be His. Be true. Be still. Let his sovereignty anchor your hopeful, fearful soul.

The story you're moving through isn't your own. Ultimately, it's not about you. Fasting should not immerse you more in your story, but less. Be unshackled. You will think of food because you are human. That's not the problem, that's just a fact of our nature. Becoming drawn into a cycle of regret that turns your vision from Jesus to yourself—that is a problem.

Thankfully, He's big enough for that problem, too.

HEALTH SMART

✦ Some people feel enervated by fasting, others feel fatigued. By now, you have likely experienced waves of both. Mileage will vary. This is normal.

VOICES OF WISDOM

✣ "Christian fasting, at its root, is the hunger of a homesickness for God."

— John Piper

REFLECTIONS

_____

_____

_____

_____

_____

_____

_____

_____

_____

_____

_____

_____

_____

_____

_____

_____

_____

_____

_____

_____

_____

_____

DAY 32

To whom then will you liken God?
Or what likeness will you compare with Him?
"To whom then will you liken Me That I should
be his equal?" says the Holy One (Isa. 40: 18, 25)

LIKE MOSES, JOB, and David before Him, Isaiah continues to elevate our understanding of God. The great prophet does this in the only way he can, by making it perfectly clear we *cannot possibly* understand Him at all! Our God is not like other gods, nor is He like us. He is *other* . . . holy. To go further than the word holy is to discover how quickly superlatives fail. Even the best language and symbolism are insufficient to bridge the gaps in our comprehension of His unfathomable splendor. If we enter the realm of poetry, He transcends it. Simile, analogy and metaphor can only help point us in the right direction, but ultimately they prove menial to the task of describing God.

So what do we do? We say things like, "Our God is a consuming fire. He is the Lion of Judah. Ancient of Days. The Chief Cornerstone." And those are all true. But still, who is He? What is He like? We know that He previously revealed Himself as a pillar of fire, a cloud by day, an ark of cherub-covered gold, flaky dew-bread in the wilderness, a rock gushing water, and numerous other prophetic pictures. Mercifully, in the fullness of time came the perfection of His final word, Jesus. And oh! How wonderful He is! But while the Son perfectly reveals the Father in clarity and truth,

He also blows the lid off our comprehension even more than all the other stuff combined. What kind of God would save His own rebellious creation by taking the punishment upon Himself in the most violent, gruesome manner imaginable?

And there you have it. To whom will you liken God? Who is His equal? What lofty new tongue must be invented that is rich enough to supply us with useful comparisons? There is none . . . because He is *incomparable*. (It is no accident that God described Himself as "the Holy One" when making this declaration).

Even so, we should not abandon the contemplation of His mystery and grandeur. Though our attempts are bound to fall short, meaningful worship occurs when we seek out creative language and imagery to consider His greatness. For me, the concept of time is instructive. Humans are bound to linear time. Each living soul gets one thin second of time called "the present" in which to operate. These flow in sequence, but only forward. Never backward. The limitations of this on our life are profound. On our best days we are capable of multitasking about four things at once, and two of those four usually turn out poorly. We get tired and grumpy if an obstacle causes a five minute detour in our day, whether that obstacle be literal traffic or figurative in the achievement of our goals. These are not merely irritations of the moment, but truly existential experiences because in the midst of them we understand with unusual clarity that we *can't* do it all; we only have so much time; our limitations define us. We have finite resources and wisdom and therefore easily become discouraged when a particular problem exceeds our capacity.

Oh boy, not the Holy One.

Being timeless—infinite in knowledge and resources—Yahweh multitasks 900,000,000,000,000 things at once, all to perfection, all before breakfast (which He doesn't bother to eat because He doesn't need it).

Yahweh multitasks 900,000,000,000,000 things at once, all to perfection. On our best day, we might muster two-dimensional thought

On our best day, we might muster two-dimensional thought. The enemy, Satan, might muster three-dimensional thought, which makes him a terrifying and diabolical genius compared to us. By contrast, the divine brilliance and energy of God operate on so many simultaneous levels it's like He's playing 16-dimensional chess on a board the size of Jupiter, with 75 quadrillion pieces. The pieces are absolutely every scrap of circumstance, coincidence and fact of history, mingled with the secret, fathomless plans of His heart, then populated with human souls—of which He knows every one by name, where they belong and what their ultimate purpose is, and whom He loves with an energy that makes the sun's fusion-powered soul seem like a half-licked lemon drop. Whew! How does He do it? Because of course, He's God. He created the board, the pieces, and His pitiful three-dimensional opponent, who doesn't stand a chance of ever thwarting one single purpose of God.

Who is like Him? None. Revel in that fact.

FAITH TIP

✓ Spend time today in adoration
prayer. Put aside your lists.
Confess your need of Him. Let
your soul adore Him. He is
unequaled in the whole
universe. Gently tell Him.
Loudly praise Him. Do not
keep silent.

VOICES OF WISDOM

✤ "Denying material food, which
nourishes our body, nurtures
an interior disposition to listen
to Christ and be fed by His
saving word. Through fasting
and praying, we allow Him to
come and satisfy the deepest
hunger that we experience in
the depths of our being: the
hunger and thirst for God."

— **Pope Benedict XVI**

REFLECTIONS

DAY 33

Lift up your eyes on high and see who has created these stars. Not one of them is missing. Why do you say, "My way is hidden from the Lord, and the justice due me escapes the notice of my God"?
(Isa. 40:26, 27)

HE WHO CREATED the stars stands ready to bring justice to His people. Justice and judgment are inextricably linked. Interestingly, while their connection is logical and plain enough, we often feel conflicted between the two. We like the idea of justice, but tend to have a more negative view of judgment. Usually, this is based in our experiences. If you have ever found yourself in stiff-necked opposition and rebellion to God—have known the sting of His correction—you might have become convinced that God is only stern and judgmental. However, as the reborn friends of God, our view must change. The judgment of God is a *good* thing!

"The judgments of the Lord are true; they are righteous altogether" (Psa. 19:9).

In His covenant with Abraham, God promised to "bless those who bless you, and those who curse you, I will curse" (Gen. 12:3). Approximately four thousand years ago, the Lord established favorable judgments on Abraham's behalf. Even more pointedly, when God spoke to the Hebrew slaves, He said, "I am the Lord, and I will bring you out from under the burdens of the Egyptians, and I will deliver you from their bondage. I will also redeem you with an outstretched arm *and with great judgments*" (Exo. 6:6; also 12:12). In other words, for Abraham and captive Israel, the judgments of God were exactly what they needed—countless blessings and no more bondage!

In our context, justice could take many forms. Healing, promotion, vindication, deliverance and mercy are just a few. God's most extravagant justice, of course, occurred 2000 years ago. Through the judgment of the Cross we are brought into the justice of God (Rom. 5:9-10; 1 Thes. 5:9-10). From that single, bedrock event God continues releasing favorable judgments on your behalf, for your good. He is *not* against us!

And yet the issue of justice creates a faith dilemma for the believer. When we are in crisis—in need of healing, deliverance, provision—we naturally cry out. This fast may represent your need of a justice breakthrough. So we dig into the Word, we find His promise for our lives, and we say, "Yes! Go God . . . and please hurry!" Because when we need deliverance, we generally need it *now.*

Unfortunately, the next agenda item isn't justice. It's delay.

Though His ways are mysterious to the natural mind, if we give in to offense, our walk will be one of perpetual defeat and ruin, believing God for nothing. Instead, God wants to teach us to overcome.

Delay brings real emotional anguish and frustration. In fact, it gets twisted inside us. We begin to feel the *in*justice of the delay more than the hope of coming salvation. Self-pity starts to creep in. We feel neglected, overlooked, uncared for. *God takes care of all these other people. They have great stories and testimonies, but not little old me. I'll just have to make it on my own, I guess.*

"My way is hidden from the Lord, and the justice due me escapes the notice of my God."

The disappointment of these moments is palpable. They are hard to bear. We easily take offense at God, and a bitter root springs up in our heart at the point of the bruise. The enemy accuses God to our minds, as if He was giggling in heaven at our torment, or withholding the justice we are due just because He feels like it that day. God is not some capricious deity straight out of the Greek pantheon, but His ways *are* mysterious to the natural mind. Offense comes naturally. If we give in, our only alternative is to walk in defeat and ruin, believing God for nothing.

This is not the way of a believer, nor the path of sonship.

In the ultimate sense—embodied in the time of His Second Coming—the desire of Jesus is not for delay, but rather to bring "speedy justice" to His elect (Luke 18:5-8). However, the clear requirement for the acceleration we seek is radical commitment to vigilant prayer. In the interim, we must be patient with delays. We live in a fallen world, and it gets pretty rough sometimes. We must have courage and fortitude. The world is a mess, but God is good.

And so we fast. We believe. We cry out for breakthrough. We persevere through the delay. Our way is no more hidden from God than the stars are hidden from the sky. Choose to believe *that*.

You are on Day 33. Keep going!

FAITH TIP

✓ Increase the time you spend
listening to the voice of the
Lord within. Your spirit craves
communication with God.
Prayer is speaking and
listening. It is conversation with
your Lord, your King, your
Beloved, your Friend.

VOICES OF WISDOM

❖ "Do you fast? Then feed the
hungry, give drink to the thirsty,
visit the sick, do not forget the
imprisoned, have pity on the
tortured, comfort those who
grieve and who weep, be
merciful, humble, kind, calm,
patient, sympathetic, forgiving,
reverent, truthful and pious, so
that God might accept your
fasting and might plentifully
grant you the fruits of
repentance."

— **St. John Chrysostom
(347-407 A.D.)**

REFLECTIONS

DAY 34

Do you not know? Have you not heard?
The Everlasting God, the Lord, the Creator of the ends
of the earth does not become weary or tired. (Isa. 40:28)

THE LAST FEW DAYS spent on the sovereignty of God is not by accident. As the time of His return draws near, the church needs to become more well-grounded than ever before in the Father's sufficiency in all things, in the extreme perfection of His governance and in His indefatigable essence. He is "the Everlasting God, the Lord, the Creator"—all titles of infinite scope, which speak of power, rulership and creativity. Other gods fail, but ours never grows weary or tired.

Isaiah frames these revelations with the question, "Have you not heard?" In other words, the evidence is all around you. Are you listening?

Why this is of such great importance in the coming days is revealed in the book of Daniel. Exiled in Babylon, Daniel had a series of prophetic revelations about the last days of earth. It is revealed to him that one of the primary strategies of the antichrist will be to "speak out against the Most High and *wear down the saints* of the Highest One" (Dan. 7:25).

To speak out against the Most High is to do what Satan has always done: accuse God. Though God is omnipotent, omniscient and omnipresent, Satan will increasingly attempt to diminish His stature and character; to make Him seem smaller, weaker, less effective, less concerned, less motivated by love. But what about the other part? Watchman Nee offers the following insight:

> "Satan has a plan against the saints of the Most High which is to wear them out. What is meant by this phrase, 'wear out'? It has in it the idea of reducing a little this minute, then reducing a little further the next minute. Reduce a little today, reduce a little tomorrow. Thus the wearing out is almost imperceptible; nevertheless, it is a reducing. The wearing down is scarcely an activity of which one is conscious, yet the end result is that there is nothing left. He will take away your prayer life little by little, and cause you to trust God less and less and yourself more and more, a little at a time. He will make you feel somewhat cleverer than before. Step by step, you are misled to rely more on your own gift, and step by step your heart is enticed away from the Lord. Now, were Satan to strike the children of God with great force at one time, they would know exactly how to resist the enemy since they would immediately recognize his work. He uses the method of gradualism to wear down the people of God."

We have not only grown content, but *dependent* on snack-sized faith. Materially, we're always striving for a little more while *becoming* a little less, trading richness of spirit for meager, impoverished photocopies of ourselves.

Like no other time in history, you and I are living witnesses of this strategy. Worse, we are servants of it. Our souls are slowly being whittled away to nothing. Intellectually, emotionally and spiritually, we feel worn and thin. We have not only grown content, but *dependent* on snack-sized faith and superficial diversions. We willingly spend our money in support of a corrupt system the Apostle John called a harlot, Babylon. We are addicted to constant stimulation; in fact, we can hardly focus without it. Our kids have to listen to their iPod to do homework and we multitask everything—job, meals, errands, soccer practice, homework, parenting, leisure time—just to survive another 24 hours before collapsing exhausted into bed that night. The next morning, we complain about the stress, but do nothing to change it. Materially, we're always striving for a little more and becoming a little less as we trade richness of spirit for meager, impoverished photocopies of ourselves. People of substance and conviction threaten us—people of prayer whose mighty Christ-filled revelation shakes the world.

We must grow effective in fasting to combat the spirit of the age with lovesick hunger.

This "gradualism" reveals why we must grow effective in fasting: to combat the spirit of the age with lovesick hunger for a God who never wearies, and therefore contains the fullness of life we seek. Not only do we seek it, we are designed and destined for it. Let us cease allowing our spiritual life to wither from the blood loss of a thousand little cuts.

Vitality comes from a hungry, relentless focus on Jesus. Are you listening?

FAITH TIP

✓ In all these many weeks of fasting, have you appropriately expressed the desperation of your heart to God? Have you wept for your breakthrough? Have you shouted to the heavens? Jericho did not fall with a whisper. Neither will some of the walls around our own hearts. Get desperate, today, in faith. Louder!

VOICES OF WISDOM

❖ "How we need the Lord to enlighten our eyes that we may comprehend afresh the importance of prayer and know anew its value. Furthermore, we must recognize that had Satan not deceived us we would not be neglecting prayer so much. We should therefore watch and discover therein all the various wiles of Satan. We will not allow him to delude us any more in relaxing in prayer . . . Our prayers lay the track down on which God's power can come. Like a mighty locomotive, his power is irresistible, but it cannot reach us without rails."

— **Watchman Nee (1903-1972)**

REFLECTIONS

_____
_____
_____
_____
_____
_____
_____
_____
_____

DAY 35

His understanding is inscrutable. (Isa. 40:28)

As YOU ENTER the home stretch of your forty days, an odd tangle of thoughts might be jangling around in your head. You could be amazed and grateful for what God has done in your life up to this point, to the point that you even dread it ending. You might feel so clean and free, so *awake* in your spirit, that returning again to "normal life" and normal diet feels like a literal drag to your soul. Yet even with such a positive frame of mind, you might wonder, *where do I go from here?* On the other hand, you might not feel satisfied or elated, you might feel disappointed. You might be thinking, *is this it?* You might have persevered in the discipline, given yourself to prayer, waited on God, and yet have no real sense of particular breakthrough. You might be discouraged. In fact, even though you have come so far, you might be tempted with thoughts like *why bother to finish?*

Let me encourage you to press through. The fact is, we simply do not see what God sees. By this I mean, our perspective is limited to whatever self-understanding we possess (which is incomplete at best) as well as the tunnel vision of linear time. Sure, we're aware of our relational ties in generic terms, but we do not readily grasp how interconnected we are to others, nor how the smallest decisions of our heart are weighed before the Lord. We're like someone trying to admire a Monet from three inches away focused on two little, blotchy brush strokes, when the real beauty of the work can only be glimpsed by stepping back far enough to take in all the elements as a whole. In other words, we're practically blind to what's really going in on in any given moment, and this doesn't even factor in the higher spiritual realities where angels and demons dwell!

You may look at your life and feel discouraged, but God looks at your heart and sees a son, a daughter, a servant, a friend. He sees a hungry, thirsty cry for more of Him or you wouldn't be here at Day 35. He treasures and *always responds* to the cry for more. It truly moves heaven and earth.

Greatness comes through smallness. Glory through weakness. Forty days is not a merit badge that qualifies you to receive God's best for your life. Quite the opposite, fasting is the systematic stripping of personal rights and power for the sake of knowing Jesus intimately.

So whether you signed up for a specific breakthrough or a general tenderizing by which you draw nearer to God, your breakthrough might come within the space of these forty day bookends, but it might not. Do not make the mistake of thinking one result is superior to the other. Here's how you finish strong. Realize you are part of an *upside-down* kingdom. Fasting turns the tables on typical "achievement" modes. Let's get real for a moment. No matter how hard you guard against it, when hope and faith pulse in your veins with Bible-inspired expectations—"This fast is going to change my life forever like it did for Moses!"—it is easy to view the journey as a form of achievement; a competitive obstacle to overcome; a persuasion tool with God, i.e. "see how good I'm being! You can trust me now!"; a checklist item with which to prove your spirituality; or a little bow-wrapped box of spiritual advancement.

Hope is good. Believing is good. It is good to knock, seek and pray . . . then keep knocking, seeking and praying. In fasting, your spirit grows strong. Naturally, faith is the result.

But in this kingdom, greatness comes through smallness. Glory comes in weakness. We lead by serving. We receive by giving away. We live by dying. Your forty days does not accumulate merit badges that somehow qualify you to receive God's best for your life. It is not the spiritual equivalent of a "Get Rich Quick" scheme on late night television. Quite the opposite, fasting is the systematic, intentional stripping of personal rights and power for the sake of knowing Jesus intimately and trusting Him more. The time lost ("wasted") in prayer, the nervous energy spent pining away for food, represent a forfeiture of the very resource which could have been marshaled to assure your success in a more worldly way. Instead, when we fast we trust the Lord to prosper us. In His time, in His way. Whether we feel it, see it or sense it at present is hardly the point. You may *never* see the direct correlation between the choices you've made over these forty days and who you will become as a result. But this is the way of God. It is backward, beyond our comprehension.

His understanding confounds us. It is inscrutable, but beautiful, really. Like a Monet.

FAITH TIP

✓ Today, fast from:
- Anger, feast on patience.
- Worry, feast on trust.
- Discontent, feast on gratitude.
- Self-concern, feast on compassion
- Bitterness, feast on forgiveness.
- Discouragement, feast on hope.
- Exaggeration, feast on honesty.
- Attention-seeking, feast on hiddenness
- Rightness, feast on agreement
- Excessive words, feast on silence.
- The future, feast on the present
- Stinginess, feast on generosity

VOICES OF WISDOM

❖ "The strictness of the *Quadragesima* (the Forty Days) mortifies the passions, extinguishes anger and rage, cools and calms every agitation springing up from gluttony. And just as in the summer, when the burning heat of the sun spreads over the earth, the northern wind renders a benefaction to those who are scorched, by dispersing the sultriness with a tender coolness: so fasting also provides the same, by driving out of bodies the burning which is the result of overeating.

— **St. Asterius of Amasia (c. 350-410)**

REFLECTIONS

_____

_____

_____

_____

_____

_____

_____

_____

_____

_____

DAY 36

He gives strength to the *weary* (Isa. 40:29)

WHILE THE DEEPER meaning of this verse is intended spiritually, Isaiah's prophecy has been proven physically during my fast. I hope the same is true for you. From about week three to the present, I have enjoyed notably higher levels of mental acuity and physical energy—more so than anytime I can think of in the last ten years. My thought processes are clearer and more focused, my body feels lighter (for good reason, having lost about 30 pounds thus far), and I have a general sense of vigor and optimism about life that has been truly wonderful to experience. I suspect this represents a synergy of the whole person being touched by fasting exactly as God intended: cleansing physically, emotionally, shedding excess weight, expanding in revelation, renewing my spirit before God.

I will tell you now, based on previous experience with extended fasting, ending the fast will almost cause a pang of loss for this very reason. Although your carnal nature hates being denied pleasure and satisfaction, your body is quite happy fasting, and your spirit absolutely thrives. Your emotions get a break from the fatigue of constant food-based stimulation, some of which even causes subtle biochemical imbalances, as in the case of unknown food allergies, etc. As a result, for all its joy, that first bite may bring a sort of letdown. Don't be afraid to eat, just be aware of this reality. Also, determine to keep a measure of the triumph of your forty days *by persevering in restraint as you begin eating again.* Ultimately, the larger goal of an extended fast is to equip your spirit to continue to deny excess consumption. As previously noted, the world is full of God-ordained pleasures and benefits. There are countless good things to be enjoyed, but we have lost our sense of propriety and moderation. We need boundaries. Let us proceed from our forty days in the mature fruit of self-control, refusing in the grace of God to gorge on legitimate pleasures with such reckless fervor that we forget God.

You are at an interesting place—physically enervated on the one hand, and yet very ready to eat again according to the normal requirements of human existence. While your spirit is made alive in the consecration of self-denial, the human frame cannot help but grow fatigued over time in the absence of food. Do not let natural urges cause you to lose your footing. Stand firm just a little while longer! Think of it it this way: if our fast can be viewed in its totality as a season of rebirth, the last few days should be even more so. Remember the *Mikveh*, the Jewish ritual bath we discussed earlier? It took forty days of rain for Noah and therefore forty units of water for cleansing. God did not stop at 35 or 36. Neither should you. Who knows what grace will be imparted in the final days, the final hours? You are entering the fullness of your own cleansing *Mikveh*. In these last few days, contend for the pleasures of the Spirit even more than fullness of flesh. This is the *creme de la creme* of your fast.

Isaiah reveals why. On the heels of establishing God's vast and total sovereignty, the conclusion of chapter 40 offers a verse-by-verse expansion of the revelation by which we ourselves enter into His strength. You have been in process. Repentance. Waiting. Humility. Honesty. Preparation. Hunger. The creation and renewal of a new identity—your true self who is "hidden with Christ in God" (Col. 3:3). The remaining days of your fast are now all about gaining new strength, new vision. A new birthing of promise lies at the threshold of your heart. Engage God-life at a new level.

After today, you only have four more days. Do not get lost in consuming thoughts of food. Be consumed with Him. Turn your energies, even your fragmented, weary devotion to the Lord with renewed vigor.

You are weary. That is good. He gives strength to the weary. You are tired. That is good. He empowers the weak.

You are empty. That is good.

Now, at last, you can be filled with divine life.

FAITH TIP

✓ Spend time today asking the Lord to experience more of His emotions of you. Ask for new revelations, new experiences of His jealousy, tenderness, compassion and joy. He delights in you. Take time to feel His love.

VOICES OF WISDOM

❖ "The more days of fasting there are, the better the healing is; the longer the period of abstinence, the more abundant the gain of salvation is."

— **St. Augustine of Hippo (354-430)**

REFLECTIONS

DAY 37

And to him who lacks might He increases power. (Isa. 40:29)

I'M GOING TO MAKE a bold claim. True, planet-shaking revival will not occur until the disciples of Jesus embrace radical fasted lifestyles. Here's why: *To him who lacks might He increases power.*

Break it down in chunks. Does the church want to increase in power? Then it must lack might. Paul said God's power "is perfected in weakness" (2 Cor. 12:9). Yet this is not how we think.

While we know that God is opposed to the proud and exalts the humble, we don't consider the full ramifications of that fact. Since pride is the anointing of Satan, everywhere God smells the stench of pride He must resist it. As such, He cannot deeply bless something infected by Satan even if every other aspect of the thing appears godly and right. He will continue to give tokens of grace because He is generous. He will continue to use weak vessels to accomplish his purpose because He is kind. His rain will still fall on just and unjust alike. But regardless the biblical soundness of a movement, if deep humility is not at the core, it cannot be sustained. Revival might come and shake a province, a region, maybe even a continent—but not the world. Why? Because at some point toxic pride will enter into the hearts of the leadership and the people. They will begin to boast, not in the Lord, but in their great consecration. They will grow proud of how mightily God is using them.

If this is a fact of revival history—and it is—how do we change it? Fasting is the surest antidote. Not a day, not a week. Not once or twice a decade. A lifestyle committed to fasting *in preparation of revival* must be reclaimed.

Long ago, fasting was not relegated to the duty of monks, but routinely practiced among all the faithful. However, during the last 500 years fasting has entered a state of general neglect. Sadly, this is probably most evident in the last 75 years of Evangelical ascendence. Just look at what we've traded for our vital spiritual energy in Christ! The American church in particular is the Catholic church of medieval times, boasting hundreds of billions worth of cumulative land and assets. We have impressive programs, great marketing and clever slogans. We have sound theology, cultural awareness, brilliant strategies, vision and political power. Best of all, everyone engaged in this work, including myself, is quite sincere. Devotion is not what's lacking. The people at the helm love Jesus and want to serve Him. What *is* lacking is the manifest power and presence of God. How did we get here? How do we get out? During a similarly barren period of Israel's history, the prophet Isaiah turned to the Lord. His prayer should be ours:

> "Awake, awake, put on strength, O arm of the
> Lord; awake as in the days of old . . . Look down from
> heaven, and see from Thy holy and glorious habitation;
> where are Thy zeal and Thy mighty deeds? . . . Oh, that
> Thou wouldst rend the heavens and come down, that
> the mountains might quake at Thy presence . . . to make
> Thy name known to Thine adversaries, that the
> nations may tremble at Thy presence! (Isa 51:9; 63:15;
> 64:1-2).

Paul declared that his message and preaching "were not in persuasive words of wisdom, but in demonstration of the Spirit and of power" (1 Cor. 2:4-5).

Would Paul even recognize our modern, affluent churches?

The good news is that a global prayer movement is emerging. The heavens are being assaulted like no other period in history with the fervent prayers of the saints. Come God, move! And He wants to. He really does! Yet in kindness He holds back. *He refuses to pour out a radical scale of anointing and power if that blessing creates the condition by which He must later oppose us.* You see, if it is true that the bigger we are the harder we fall, what's not said is that we usually fall because God Himself has tripped us! Pride not only causes countless personal blind spots, it demands the terrifying, direct opposition of an omnipotent God. He is ruthlessly committed to oppose the chief characteristic of Satan wherever it is found . . . especially in His own people.

Contrast this with fasting, which is *voluntary weakness*. No spiritual discipline (not Bible Study, prayer, worship, tithing or ministry to the poor) so directly connects our hearts (not just heads) to weakness as fasting. To humble and restrain our flesh is to humble and restrain our pride. No, we do not kill pride with fasting. If we did, *that* would make us proud! Instead, we painfully recognize its prevalence in our lives. Brokenhearted, we confess our need and tenderly cling to the Lord. In this way, fasting sustains true, lasting humility.

Such humility will enable unbridled revival, divinely authorized rather than divinely opposed.

FAITH TIP

✓ Pride will rear it's ugly head at different points: "I'm a super-saint" kind of pride, because you are fasting. Reject such foolishness. We fast because we are needy.

VOICES OF WISDOM

❖ "Every request needs humility of spirit. Fast then, and you will receive from the Lord what you ask."

— Hermas the Shepherd (55-150)

REFLECTIONS

_____

_____

_____

_____

_____

_____

_____

_____

_____

_____

_____

_____

_____

_____

_____

_____

_____

_____

DAY 38

Those who wait for the Lord will gain new strength
(Isa. 40:30-31)

NOTICE HOW MANY times we've seen words related to *wait* and *weary* in Psalms 40 and Isaiah 40. It is a recurrent theme. Having come to the end of our journey, in need of new strength, we are given a promise; therefore we must wait. Were there not a time delay between our pledge and it's fulfillment, the sacred Word would be no Promise at all, but merely an Announcement: "Here it is!" To wait is to grow in patience, "And thus, having patiently waited, he obtained the promise" (Heb. 6:15). When we mature in patience, we mature in the Holy Spirit. We become *eternalized*. Fittingly, the word 'patience' is better rendered 'endurance' in most instances in Scripture, at least according to our English understanding of those two words. This is key as we consider the purpose of waiting.

Since patience exists on a continuum, it is appropriate that we've come full circle over the course of our forty days together. Having begun with waiting, we now end with waiting. Developing patience is one of the primary operations of the Holy Spirit in man, as He stretches our mortal into immortality. Get used to it, friend. The conclusion of one waiting cycle will only begin a new one. While that may sound discouraging (because waiting is almost always difficult), incomparable richness is transferred to your soul through this process.

Why is it so important that we learn how to wait? The answer drives us once more into the arms of a wholly *other* God, Who thinks differently than us in every way. He is not afraid of our weaknesses, as we are, nor is He intimidated by the passage of time. It makes no difference to Him, a little time, a lot of time. He feels none of our anxiety when something is taking too long. This is because He is eternal, a fact which translates roughly thus: Time has no power over Him.

To say that Time has no power over God means that He does not age, wrinkle or grow frail. He doesn't have arthritis or heart problems. Obvious, right? But it is no more false than claiming He is ever young, because such a claim only misses the point from the other end. No, God simply *is.* That's the mystery of His great pronouncement, *I Am.* His exalted name is a self-referencing word, for God can only reference Himself to explain Himself; nothing else will do. He is not old or young. Those words only have meaning to we who live as prisoners of the passage of time. He on the other hand is Eternal. Time is to God what a canvas is to an artist, or a piece of plain white paper is to a writer. It is the medium in which He tells His story. It is an artifice, a created device.

Stage left, enter the beauty of patience. Since we are commanded in all things to "be perfect as your heavenly Father is perfect" (Mat. 5:48), the true disciple understands than every aspect of God's power and virtue is meant to increasingly manifest in our lives. We are to behold Him and become Him, meaning we put Him on display with our very existence. That's what a disciple does, increasingly conform to the image of the Master. We become like Jesus, who Himself perfectly embodied the Father. The Father is eternal.

So how do you embody and display eternity? Humans are by definition *not* eternal. We are mortal, trapped within the confines of linear Time. True, our spirit and soul are eternal, but they are immaterial entities. Becoming like Jesus is a *lived* experience, meaning we are meant to incarnate Him in the flesh as He did the Father. These become nearly irreconcilable, since our physical existence has a shelf-life, after which we expire. Our reactions, urgencies and schedules are all born out of the hourglass reality. It is a fact of life: we only have 24 hours in a day, 365 days a year, and no guarantee of tomorrow. How does a limited creature of such obvious restraints emulate and demonstrate the eternal qualities of a timeless God?

In a word, patience.

Time has no mastery over the man or woman who possesses a patient spirit.

Remember, a good working definition of the eternal nature of God is that Time has no power over Him. Likewise, *Time has no mastery over the man or woman who possesses a patient spirit.* The urgent loses its urgency. Schedules no longer make us uptight. Lines at Wal-Mart don't ruin our day and crisis shrinks to a breakthrough on pause. We abide in the flow of His eternal peace. We contend for the promise with prayer and waiting. In so doing, we liberate ourselves from oppressive fears. We gain new strength. It is no mystery that one of the fruits of the Holy Spirit—divine qualities expressed in human terms—is patience. By patient endurance we are eternalized.

FAITH TIP

✓ What if Noah had lost his patience building the ark and stopped 6 months early? Or consider 400 years in bondage for the Hebrew slaves. After 399 years, they still didn't know God's timing. Would the deliverer *ever* arrive? Yet God did it. Meditate on His faithfulness today. He is committed to you.

VOICES OF WISDOM

❖ "Fasting is the soul of prayer; mercy is the lifeblood of fasting. So, if you pray, fast; if you fast, show mercy. If you want your petition to be heard, hear the petition of others. If you do not close your ear to other, you open God's ear to yourself."

— St. Peter Chrysologus (380– 450)

REFLECTIONS

_____

_____

_____

_____

_____

_____

_____

_____

_____

_____

_____

_____

_____

_____

_____

_____

DAY 39

They will mount up with wings like eagles (Isa. 40:32)

Ahh, NOW IT IS time to soar! For this you have fasted, that you might "mount up with wings."

This is primarily metaphoric language for revelation; secondarily for the triumph, abundant life which results from expanding vision. An eagle sees panoramically, vast swathes, miles of earth at a time. In more practical terms, when a criminal is being pursued, foot traffic and cop cars are insufficient. That's why they put a "bird" in the air; a helicopter. The thief is apprehended. Over the past four decades, hundreds of satellites costing billions of dollars have been launched into low, geostationary or medium earth orbit, enabling everyone from the military to Google to help us see things we've never seen before. These "birds" in the sky provide everything from intelligence for national security to useful business information, ecological and meteorological data, to communication and personal assistance in the form of GPS turn-by-turn navigation when you're traveling to a new city. In other words, with the assistance of higher vision, *you don't get lost, you stay safe, you prosper.*

If this is true in the natural, how much more when the Spirit beckons us to higher dimensions? To receive the mind-blowing spectacle of the Apocalypse, John the Beloved was told, "Come up here!" (Rev. 4:1). He looked and beheld a door standing open in the high places of heaven. Immediately (vs. 2), he was caught up "in the spirit". He couldn't stay earth-bound and see what he needed to see. He had to move to a higher dimension. He needed new vision.

Solomon taught God's people to continually stand in fresh revelation lest they drift into danger and even perish (Prov. 29:18, KJV). Others translations help us understand what this means: "Where there is no prophetic vision (ESV) . . . no revelation, the people cast off restraint" (NIV). Interestingly, Young's Literal Translation says, "Without a Vision is a people made naked." Jeremiah wept when the devastation of Judah proved Solomon's warning: "Her gates have sunk into the ground . . . the law is no more; also, her prophets find no vision from the Lord" (Lam. 2:9).

The implication is clear. When we lose our vision, our soul drifts freely toward countless destructive pursuits. Adam lost his vision of the Tree of Life. Moses lost his vision of the Promised Land, becoming more focused on the frustrations of leading a rebellious people. In anger, he struck the rock. Peter focused on the storm instead of Jesus and began to sink beneath the water. By contrast, gaining true revelation fascinates and compels us to pursue the noble truth we have witnessed. Like the Gadarene demoniac touched by Christ, we become clothed and in our right mind. We are no longer naked, purposeless, on the edge of destruction.

They shall renew strength . . . and mount up . . . like eagles.

We see this reality evidenced in the mystical imagery of the Cherubim and Seraphim before the Throne Room of God. There is no higher revelation of God than seated on His throne. He alone is the focus, the epicenter of fascination. Nothing else is worthy of attention. Is it any wonder that the Cherubim of Ezekiel 10 and the Seraphim of Revelation 4 are described as being "full of eyes?"

> "And as for their appearance, all four of them had the same likeness, as if one wheel were within another wheel. When they moved, they went in any of their four directions without turning as they went; but they followed in the direction which they faced, without turning as they went. And their whole body, their backs,

their hands, their wings, and the wheels were full of eyes all around" (Eze. 10:10-12).

The imagery is striking: Eyes and wings. Eyes and wings.

There is no higher revelation than God on His throne. He the epicenter of fascination.

Do you see the pattern? Elevation + Revelation. Soaring brings sight. There can be no higher place than to stand in the undiluted splendor of the heavenly throne room where God is revealed in His totality. Flesh cannot survive there, nor sin. All is perfection and beauty. No veils, no masks. Thus, the four Living Creatures are "full of eyes around and within" (Rev. 4:8) as they ever gaze upon the beauty of God. Whether mystically or literally, it seems two eye are insufficient to drink it all in.

Of course, this is not an automatic process, like flipping a switch. Yet in denying fleshly desires we have sought to elevate spiritual desire according to the pattern of Scripture. In fasting, it is only fitting to yearn for a deeper, higher revelation of Christ. For the last several weeks you have been on a journey of fresh revelation. One more day and your forty days is complete.

FAITH TIP

✓ As your 40 days comes to a close, remember, repentance is not the complex process of emotional mortification we often make it. It is far more simple: *change your mind!* When that truly happens, actions will follow. Today, allow your thoughts to shift away from lukewarm, passive attitudes regarding eternity. Do not succumb to the immediacy and dullness of the been-there-done-that culture. When the cynicism of this age inevitably rubs off on us, it only proves our need for ongoing personal awakening. Allow God to continue His work of humility, passion and conviction in your soul. We *always need more* of Him! Give Him permission to relentlessly complete His work.

VOICES OF WISDOM

✤ " Let thy mind fast from vain thoughts; let thy memory fast from remembering evil; let thy will fast from evil desire; let thine eyes fast from bad sights: turn away thine eyes that thou mayest not see vanity; let thine ears fast from vile songs and slanderous whispers; let thy tongue fast from slander, condemnation, blasphemy, falsehood, deception, foul language and every idle and rotten word; let thy hands fast from killing and from stealing another's goods; let thy legs fast from going to evil deeds: Turn away from evil, and do good.

— **St. Tikhon of Zadonsk (1724-1783)**

REFLECTIONS

_____

_____

_____

_____

_____

_____

_____

_____

_____

_____

DAY 40

They will run and not grow weary,
they will walk and not faint. (Isa. 40:32)

ONE WELL-KNOWN rule of biblical interpretation is called the Principle of First Occurrence. This rule states that the first appearance of a particular word or term in the Bible often holds unique insights for the application of subsequent uses of that word throughout the remainder of Scripture. Theologically rich words like *covenant, atonement, sacrifice, mercy, prophet, law,* etc. all have a first occurrence that is meaningful in setting the stage for future understanding. It is thus instructive that 40 is first mentioned during Noah's forty days and nights. Though we have already studied this, it continues to inform our journey to the very last day. An orthodox Jew might add: "Sof Maaseh b'machshavas tehilla," which means *the end result comes from the first thought.*

Let us examine God's "first thought" regarding the purpose of forty and apply this revelation to our own ending. During the last six weeks, you have consecrated yourself unto the Lord in hopes of *repentance* and *rebirth.* Like Noah, we have experienced our own "earth cleansing". Noah emerged from the ark to a world scrubbed clean of sin and defilement. It was a fresh start, a form of new birth. Noah's ordeal speaks of our own salvation—the cleansing flow, the baptism into water and Spirit—realized in the grace of Christ. But it is also expressed in the newness of life cultivated by the furnace and flood of fasting. The water of the Word has been applied to our minds in forty measures. In voluntary weakness, we have built an altar to the Lord forty stones tall, one day at a time. We have consecrated ourselves before His faithful, searching gaze, that He might try our hearts and refine our motives. In this span of time, we have run headlong into the weakness of our cold hearts. We have discovered how easily we fill our bellies with other pleasures and offer our affections to other gods. With appropriate grief, we have cried out. We have chosen not passivity, but fervency, like John the Baptist preparing a highway of holiness for the glory of the Lord within. Like the Apostle Paul who said, "I treat my body hard and make it my slave so that I myself will not be disqualified" (1 Cor. 9:27), we have disciplined our stubborn flesh for the purpose of knowing Christ's pleasures above enslavement to excess.

No doubt, you have felt weary along the way. Take heart. Now comes the rebirthing, the surge of new life! Knowing, trusting in the promise of God, you have waited for His salvation, and He has drawn you higher with wings of the Spirit. The Holy Spirit testifies that when you reach the end of yourself *you have not reached the end of Him.* Therefore, "you will run and not grow weary" because you have tapped into a deeper source of life. A season of new revelation has come.

Does all this happen at once? No, it unfolds. There is more to come. But there is a new, clean place within. Trust God in that place. Enjoy the gift He only gives to the hungry.

"Blessed are those who hunger and thirst for righteousness, for they shall be satisfied" (Mat. 5:6). That word 'satisfied' means *filled.* You have been empty. Now be filled with God.

This is not the end. Forty days and forty nights was not the end for Noah, it was the beginning. We, too, stand ready to be commissioned for a lifestyle of hunger and restraint.

This part of your journey is complete. Well done. Now press on. There is more, always more, of Him. "So let us know, let us press on to know the Lord. His going forth is as certain as the dawn;

And He will come to us like the rain, like the spring rain watering the earth" (Hos. 6:3).

Prayer: *Holy Spirit, fill us anew! Grant us abiding passion for Jesus, newness of life and renewed dedication to establishing the Kingdom of God on earth. Let us be faithful to prepare the way for the coming King! Let beauty and holiness be demonstrated in our lives with power. Consecrate us for the full pleasure and purpose of God in our generation. Amen!*

HEALTH SMART

✦ It is *critical* that you ease back into solid foods as you resume a more regular diet! Wisdom and self-control are crucial for good health. Also, use the opportunity of your fast to establish smarter eating habits and smaller portions. Please see 'Appendix E' for further recommendations on how to gradually transition back to eating.

VOICES OF WISDOM

❖ "Fasting possesses great power. If practiced with the right intention, it makes one a friend of God. The demons are aware of that."

— Quintus Tertullian (160-220)

REFLECTIONS

_____

_____

_____

_____

_____

_____

_____

_____

Review of Insights From My 40 Days with Christ

_____

_____

_____

_____

_____

_____

_____

_____

_____

_____

_____

_____

_____

_____

_____

_____

_____

_____

_____

_____

_____

_____

_____

_____

_____

APPENDIX A

A Non-Exhaustive List of Occurrences of the Number '40' in Scripture & Nature

1. During Noah's flood, it rained for 40 days and 40 nights.
   - Note: the Hebrew letter *mem*, whose name is from *mayim* (meaning water or fluid in general), also equals 40 according to Hebrew gematria.
2. Noah waited another 40 days after the rain stopped before he opened a window in the Ark.
3. The Egyptians embalmed Joseph and the people mourned 40 days as per their custom.
4. Isaac was 40 years old when he took Rebekah to wife
5. Moses' life is divided into three stages of 40:
   - At age 40, he killed the Egyptian and fled to the wilderness.
   - He remained in the desert 40 more years before receiving God's call at age 80 to return to Egypt as Israel's deliverer.
   - He spent the last 40 years of his life leading Israel through the wilderness, dying at 120.
6. Moses was with the Lord on Mt. Sinai 40 days when he first received the 10 Commandments.
7. Moses spent a second 40 days of prayer and fasting on Mount Sinai to receive the Law a second time, after the original tablets were destroyed in the judgment of the golden calf.
8. Forty lashes was prescribed as punishment for the guilty in civil disputes (Deut. 25:3)
9. Joshua was 40 years old when Moses assigned him to go into Jericho as a spy.
10. The 12 spies investigated the land for 40 days before reporting back to Moses.

11. As penalty for their unbelief, the Israelites wandered through the the wilderness for 40 years, one year for every day the original spies had been in the land. After 40 years were complete, Joshua led the Children of Israel across Jordan and took Jericho.

12. When Israel did not obey God, He delivered them to Philistine control for 40 years

13. In the time of the Judges, after periods of repentance, the land was given rest 40 years at a time. (Judges 3:11, 5:31, 8:28)

14. Samuel judged Israel 40 years

15. King Saul reigned for 40 years.

16. Goliath taunted Saul and the army of Israel 40 days before being killed by David.

17. King David reigned for 40 years.

18. King Solomon reigned for 40 years.

19. Elijah journeyed 40 days to Mount Horeb where he heard the voice of God

20. Ezekiel lay for 40 days on his left side as a prophetic sign for the 40 years of iniquity of the children of Israel.

21. In Ezekiel's time, the land was desolate for 40 years.

22. Jonah warned the City of Nineveh they had 40 days until God would overthrow the city.

23. After giving birth, a Jewish woman was to enter a 40 day period called the Days of Purification (Lev. 12:1-8). In keeping with the Law of Moses, Jesus was presented at the temple following Mary's days of purification (Luke 2:21-22).

24. Prior to beginning His public ministry, Jesus fasted 40 days in the wilderness.

25. Before ascending to Heaven, Jesus was seen in the earth 40 days after His resurrection

26. Forty years after Jesus' crucifixion, Jerusalem fell to Rome.

27. The normal gestational period of a baby is 40 weeks.

28. In Jewish tradition, the soul enters the fetus 40 days after conception

APPENDIX B
A Non-Exhaustive List of Biblical Examples of Fasting

1. God's people fasted to request His aid in crisis or wartime (as a nation), when loved ones were sick (David), in seeking God's forgiveness for themselves and their nation (Ahab, Daniel), and in seeking God's protection and will (Ezra).

2. Fasting is mentioned in general numerous times, among them: Lev 16:29-31; 23:26-32; Num. 29:7; Psalm 69:10; Acts 27:9. Fasting was accompanied by prayer (Psalm 35:13), penance (1 Kings 21:27), and seeking God earnestly (2 Sam. 1:12).

3. Forty day fasts were practiced by Moses, Elijah, and Jesus himself. Fasting was not only for the leaders, but was practiced commonly at various times (Deut. 9:15-18; Judges 20:26; 1 Kings 21:27).

4. Israel fasted at Bethel, in the war against the Benjamites at Mizpah, and in the Philistine war (Judges 20:26; 1 Sam 7:6). In the book of Ruth, the entire nation fasted when they discovered Haman's plot to wipe them out (Esther 4:3-16).

5. David fasted for Saul and Jonathan, for his son while he was dying, and for his enemies (2 Sam. 1:12; 2 Sam. 12:16-23; Psalm 35:11-13). Daniel fasted for Israel (Dan. 9:3-5).

6. Combining fasting with prayer humbles us (Psalm 35:13); it also disciplines and corrects wrong behaviors and thinking (Psalm 69:10), and also causes God to attend to our prayers (Ezra 8:21-23). Fasting is meant to be accompanied by loving service and concern for the poor, turning from wickedness, and acts of

justice for the oppressed as the precursor to great revival (Isa. 58:3-8).

7. In the New Testament, fasting was practiced when one was faced with temptations (Jesus), in serving God and beginning a new ministry (Antioch), and, when selecting and appointing elders (Matt. 4:1-2).

8. John the Baptist regularly fasted (Matt. 3:11). Paul listed fasting among the things that proved he was a valid, trustworthy minister of Christ (1 Cor. 11:1; 2 Cor. 11:23-28). The early church practiced fasting as they further sought God's will, drawing them deeper into His presence (Acts 13:2-3; 14:21-23).

APPENDIX C
Health Concerns

The following observations relate primarily to a juice fast.

As you launch into the current 40-day fast, or plan future extended fasts (of 10 days or more), a few general guidelines will help maximize your experience and minimize negative *incidental* health effects. I emphasize incidental because the merits of fasting are, on the whole, far more advantageous for your health than you might have previously thought. However, a little wisdom goes a long way in developing a lifestyle of fasting. Though I have completed 20- and 40-day fasts in the past, I did not truly do it "right" until this one. On previous fasts, my chosen discipline involved a single piece of dry bread and numerous glasses of 100% grape juice off the grocery store shelf, plus additional glasses of water. There are two problems with this:

1. A bottled fruit juice (typically from concentrate) is extremely high in sugar. As such, it is little better than soda. The health benefits of processed fruit juice are negligible compared to fresh juice from raw fruits and vegetables. This is because the essential nutrients and (more importantly) *natural enzymes* that are a part of the raw fruit—which help your body process the sugar and absorb the nutrients—have long since vanished in the processing. Avoid this if at all possible.

2. Furthermore, not understanding the body efficiencies generated in a low-carb, *ketogenic* cycle, my well-intentioned daily process of communion was actually filling my system with high, empty carb content, which was not only detrimental physically but I also believe offset some of the spiritual intentions of the fast. These were good fasts in terms of self-denial and restraint, but my body

never gained the benefit of ketosis. While ketosis is a fairly new medical concept, I feel certain it is another validation of the ancient wisdom of fasting, ordained by God to benefit spirit, soul *and body*. In summary, although my early attempts were no less sincere, they were unwise. *(For more information, google "Fasting and ketosis." Also see 'Appendix D' #5: Cleansing).*

In addition to the cautions listed above, I would also note the following. Some of these are included in greater detail the daily meditations; I summarize them here for easy review:

- Stay hydrated. Drink 6-8 full glasses of water a day. Purified water is even better.

- During an extended fast, you may feel shaky or weak at different points of the day. Blood sugar issues vary from person to person and will likely be in flux until your body finds a new equilibrium. This can be uncomfortable, but is rarely serious. To offset these effects, consider taking a teaspoon of peanut butter once or twice a day. The extra protein will help.

- Light to medium walking is a good idea, but on a forty day juice or water fast, heavy exercise is not advised.

- Consider a good quality herbal tea as part of the fluids you drink. A variety of good "cleanser" formulations can be found at any reputable health food store. Prepare these plain and sip a cup or two a day in addition to the water you consume. These will help strengthen the kidneys and liver as they labor to cleanse the blood and renew the body.

- A variety of common side effects can include: headaches (from caffeine withdrawal, et al), dry, cracked lips, dizziness, heartburn, slightly blurred vision, skin rashes, coldness (due to blood sugar fluctuations and fat loss) and, of course, fatigue. Fuzzy, unfocused thinking can also occur. Generalized aches and pains might surface in various regions of the body, often where the body is working to restore itself. These admittedly unpleasant feelings are rarely serious, usually temporary, and often a good sign that your body is restoring itself.

- As fasting detoxifies your body, it is natural to experience a period of unusual body odor and unpleasant tastes—perhaps even a coating—on the tongue. These could vary from minor to foul, depending on your particular health profile.

- You will likely feel more tired than normal at the end of the day. Get plenty of rest.

- Although your intestines will enter a sort of hibernation period, raw juicing with something like a Champion juicer can slowly accumulate enough trace amounts of pulp in your digestive tract to produce an occasional bowel movement (perhaps once every week or two). For this reason, it is important that you consume adequate fluids in between your morning, noon and evening juice. Why? Not only does your system need the hydration in general, and not only does it facilitate good cleansing, but if you fail to drink 6-10 glasses of fluid a day (including juice), constipation can occur. Under the unusual conditions of an extended fast, this constipation can lend itself to the development of hemorrhoids. Obviously, you would be wise to avoid this at all cost! Drink water!

APPENDIX D
My Routine During This Fast

In the hopes of generating a groundswell of interest in 40-day fasts among believers, I felt it might be helpful to share my own routine. This is by no means the only way of structuring your fast, but it might serve as a guide around which you can creatively build your own.

1. Juicing — I used a Champion juicer twice a day (lunch and dinner), producing an average of 6-10 ounces of juice per drink. I tried to buy organic if at all possible. Just about any fruits were fair game, but my vegetable juice consisted mainly of carrots, celery and beet, with a hint of lime. One veggie juice and one fruit juice a day. The juice can be nominally filling, but barely enough to knock off the edge. Just don't make a meal of it or you'll rob yourself of the fast. However, the raw properties of the juice are incredibly healthy for you.

2. Water — As the fast progressed, I began skipping a lunch or dinner juicing, substituting only water instead. During the last twenty days, I drank water nearly as much as I juiced, including one six day stretch of water alone. Of course, even while juicing, I drank multiple glasses of water a day.

3. Prayer — Being proximal to the International House of Prayer missions base in Kansas City, Missouri afforded me a certain flexibility in my routine that won't be feasible for most. But whatever your return, you can be creative. Basically, I tried to carve out several hours a day for prayer, meditation and time in the Word. Typically, I achieved about half my allotted time per day, and even some of that was unfruitful. It takes practice to focus your thoughts, to not get distracted, to bring your heart before the Lord and engage Him day after day. Don't be timid. Set a big goal for yourself. Rise earlier than normal if necessary, while also maximizing your "in between" times, meal breaks, etc. As much as you are able, consecrate the space necessary to enrich yourself in His presence. It will be easy to find excuses, to grow lax, but for six weeks, press in with a diligent spirit. You are fasting for a reason. What is it? Make the most of your forty days.

4. **Energy** — Early in the fast, as my body adjusted to the drastic reduction of intake, I would take a teaspoon or two of peanut butter along with my juicings. In such small doses, the protein content is minimal, but might be helpful for those who feel shaky or weak. Depending on your needs, raw almond or sunflower seed butter might be an even healthier alternative.

5. **Cleansing** — In his nutritional blog, ProteinPower.com, Dr. Michael Eades offers a summary of the latest medical literature covering the cellular cleansing action of a fast:

> "Anti-aging scientists are now pretty sure that one of the forces behind the aging and senescence process is the junk protein matter that accumulates in the cells, hampering cellular function. If the junk builds up enough, it basically crowds out the working part of the cell, killing the cell off in the process. As this inexorable process proceeds, more and more cells function less and less well until we, as a being, cease to function. There are other processes driving the aging function besides this accumulation of cellular debris, but if we can make some headway with cleaning out the junk, then we should be able to make the cells, and by extension us, function better for longer.

> "We have little chemically-operated waste disposal systems in our cells called lysosomes. Cellular

debris that gets hauled to the lysosomes and dumped in gets degraded into individual amino acids, which are released into the circulation and used to re-synthesize other, functional, proteins. The process of transporting the junk proteins to the lysosomes is handled by enzymes designed for that purpose found within the cells. As long as the enzymes are working up to snuff, the junk doesn't accumulate. But as the *Nature* paper shows, the aging process takes its toll. Random errors in protein synthesis of these enzymes due to the aging process means that some end up being functional while others aren't. The non-functional enzymes then not only don't help haul the junk to the lysosomes, they themselves become junk. It's easy to see what's going to happen as time marches on ...

"(To slow this process and de-junk our cells) . . . ketosis sends a message that the body needs to conserve both glucose and protein. The body begins to conserve glucose by signaling to many of the organs and tissues to start using ketones for energy instead of glucose. The body conserves protein by decreasing its use of glucose because in the absence of dietary carbohydrate (as in starvation) the body makes glucose out of protein. Conserving glucose by switching to ketones allows the body can preserve its protein stores. The other thing the body can do is to make sure that the protein it does break down to use for glucose formation comes from non-essential sources. What more non-essential source can we have than useless junk proteins floating around in the cells?"

Since fasting naturally cleanses the body by scouring junk proteins that build-up in your body's cells, I decided to help the process indirectly through the addition of what are generically called Supergreens. Although there are many on the market, I would recommend Garden of Life's *Perfect Food - Super Green Formula* or Vibrant Health's *Green Vibrance*. These nutritionally dense foods contain a mix of items like spirulina, kelp, seaweed, barley grass, wheat grass, alfalfa, etc. They come in powdered form and are meant to be stirred into water and drunk. The content is not filling; it is really no different than the other glasses of water, except for the unpleasant taste. The payoff is significant not only as an energy boost, but in supplying your cells with carotenoids, phytonutrients, amino acids and trace minerals that are simply not a part of our standard diet. In addition, you can add things like fish oils, flaxseed oil, a good quality multivitamin and herbal teas designed to strengthen and stimulate the eliminatory organs (especially the kidney and liver).

6. Rest — By the end of the day, you will likely melt into your bed. Energy may be boosted during the day. Don't push the natural limits of the weakness of a fast. You need your rest!

7. Ending the Fast — This is important. You do *not* want to rush the transition back to normal food consumption. Not only is it unwise, it could be dangerous to your health. You have to "wake up" your system slowly, train it back to foods, and generally move at a guarded, careful pace. Resist the urge to "celebrate" the completion of your fast by bingeing on your favorite foods. Not only does this reckless lust for food contradict the spirit of the fast, it forces your body to deal suddenly with food materials it has learned to do without and, in some respects, no longer misses. You should plan a 7-14 day exit strategy beyond your fast. A careful, disciplined transition plan is vital to successfully completing your fast. My exit looked something like this:

Days 1-3: Broth made from boiling the peelings of potato skins, carrot skins, chopped celery, garlic and onions. This broth is rich in potassium and other trace minerals, but easy on the system.

Days 4-5: Rather than juice only, prepare blended, all-fruit smoothies. This adds easily digestible pulp to your limited diet.

Days 6-10: Whole, raw fruits and vegetables are next; also, thin vegetable soups with minimal chunks and no meat; maybe a half slice of bread toward the end of this period of time. Chew methodically. *Over*chew.

Days 11-14: Soup and salad, with variety. Add in small meat portions if you like, preferably chicken or fish. Keep chewing well.

Days 15+: Your transition is basically complete, just be cautious with any additions of heavy, greasy foods or portions that are too large. Of course, this is generally good counsel whether fasting or not. Keep eating raw fruits and vegetables.

APPENDIX E

Other Fasting Resources

BOOKS

- *The Rewards of Fasting: Experiencing the Power and Affections of God* by **Mike Bickle and Dana Candler**

- *Fasting: Opening the Door to a More Intimate Relationship with God* by **Jentezen Franklin**

- *Fasting and Eating for Health: A Medical Doctor's Program for Conquering Disease* by **Joel Fuhrman and Neal D. Barnard**

- *Fasting: The Ancient Practices* by **Scot McKnight**

- *Fasting for Spiritual Breakthrough: A Guide to Nine Biblical Fasts* by **Elmer L. Towns**

- *Fasting: Spiritual Freedom Beyond Our Appetites* by **Lynne M. Baab**

- *The Fasting Handbook: Dining from an Empty Bowl* by **Jeremy Safron**

- *The Hidden Power of Prayer and Fasting* by **Mahesh Chavda**

WEBSITES

- **ccci.org/training-and-growth** (look for "Fasting")

- **freedomyou.com** (click on "Fasting Center")

Other books by Dean Briggs

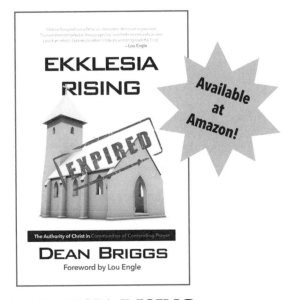

EKKLESIA RISING
The Authority of Christ in Communities of Contending Prayer

"Hard-hitting, brilliant exposition. *Ekklesia Rising* will fuel a flame of intercessory dominion in your soul. The revelation contained in these pages has launched me into a whole new paradigm of prayer. Let the ekklesia arise!" **– Lou Engle**

Fiction

"Fiction for Heroes"
The Legends of Karac Tor

Forty Days & Forty Nights
Songs of Contemplation and Intimacy

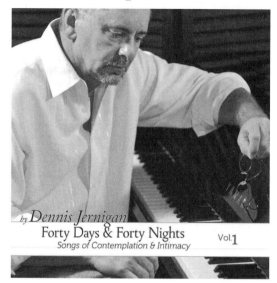

SPECIAL OFFER!

Deepen the richness and impact of your fast with these beautiful songs of contemplation and worship composed by renowned worship leader Dennis Jernigan during his own 40-day journey. Inspired by *Consumed*, every song is themed in harmony with the daily meditations to perfectly express your soul's hunger for more of God. **Incl. 40 songs.**

If you bought *Consumed* through Amazon, you can get the entire song collection embedded in the <u>Kindle version for only $2.99</u> (80% off).

This 40-song, 4-volume companion collection can be purchased separately at DennisJernigan.com

Partners in Ministry

EKKLESIA
Prayer Communities

Our motto is our mission: *Joining Heaven and Earth, together.* We are a nationwide family of contending prayer that stands in His righteousness, rather than striving to prove our own. Anchored by covenant and community, we believe that transformation happens on earth when the ekklesia exercises revelation and authority in contending prayer. **Go to <u>GoEPC.org</u> for more info.**

MoravianWatch.com

The Moravian Watch is nothing less than a new model of 24/7 prayer designed to strengthen every house, especially smaller HOPs. We believe small is the new big. As such, the Watch is a restoration of the prime mission and constitution of ekklesia. Utilizing zero cost, off-the-shelf video conferencing technology, we want to expand the prayer culture by coordinating friendship and face-to-face togetherness in prayer via videoconferencing to leverage the vast power of 2 or 3. The Holy Spirit is joyfully rebirthing new Moravian communities.

Go to <u>MoravianWatch.com</u> for more info.

ABOUT THE AUTHOR

Dean Briggs is a husband, father, teacher and intercessor.
He leads the Ekklesia Prayer Communities (EPC) network of
contending prayer. For more information on EPC's Moravian Watch
initiative, visit GoEPC.org. Dean is also a trainer at the Spiritual Air
Force Academy (SAFA) on the campus of the US Center for World
Missions in Pasadena, CA. He is married and has eight children.
Go to DeanBriggs.com for more info.